RETIREMENT

CLUES FOR THE CLUELESS

CHRISTOPHER D. HUDSON
DENISE KOHLMEYER
MARY ANN LACKLAND
RANDY SOUTHERN
CAROL SMITH
LINDA TAYLOR

PROMISE
PRESS
An Imprint of Barbour Publishing

Developed and produced by the Livingstone Corporation.

Interior Design by Design Corps, Batavia, IL.

Cover Design by Robyn Martins.

Cover and Interior Artwork by Elwood Smith.

ISBN: 1-57748-565-3

Published by: Promise Press, an imprint of Barbour Publishing, Inc., P.O. Box 719
                  Uhrichsville, OH 44683.

Printed in the United States of America.

TABLE OF CONTENTS

··

INTRODUCTION

How much money do you need to retire?
What should you do to prepare for retirement?
Where should you live when you retire?
How will retirement affect your family?
What will you do with your new free time?

The answers to these questions are different for everybody. Your age, health, occupation, interests, and family status will affect your answers. The good news, though, is that there *are* answers.

Whether you're retired or not, this book can help. It will help you budget and manage your money, plan your health care, and—most importantly—enjoy a fulfilling retirement.

While the answers to your questions may not be easy, this book will give you the clues you need to find them. You'll find out where to look and whom to ask. You'll find phone numbers, companies, and web sites that will give you the information you need. If you need it to retire, you'll probably find information about it here. Inside you'll find:

CATCH A CLUE

A Truckload of Clues. You'll learn tips from people who have successfully prepared for retirement and enjoyed it. You'll find clues to assist your own retirement.

WIDE ANGLE

Perspective. We easily get caught up in the details of day-to-day living. To best prepare for retirement, though, we sometimes need help looking at the whole picture. We'll help you take a step back.

WOW!

Amazing Stories and Facts. Getting ready for retirement can produce some fascinating stories. We've collected a few choice pieces for you to enjoy.

DON'T FORGET

Important Reminders. Certain things are important to remember as you retire or prepare for it. We've high-lighted those for you.

THE BOTTOM LINE

The Bottom Line. We'll help you get beyond confusion by letting you know the most important stuff to remember.

THE BIBLE SAYS

Help from Above. We've highlighted a few key verses that will help you understand what the Bible has to say about your retirement.

Preparing for retirement does not need to overwhelm or confuse you any longer. The questions you have are ready to be answered. There's just one thing you need to do: *Read this book.* Feel free to read it *your* way: from cover to cover or skipping around to the parts that interest you most. No matter how you read it, you'll find it's jammed with good advice, great ideas, and entertaining thoughts. So turn the page and start reading. . . . You'll be glad you did!

SECTION 1
BEYOND RETIREMENT

SEARCH FOR THE HOLY GRAIL

Ready for retirement? Some people *really* look forward to it:

> I can finally spend time with my grandchildren and family! I'll have them over every weekend for supper and let's see. . .we'll make cookies and paper dolls until the cows come home! Why, we might even turn the garage out back into a guest house. . .they could live right here with us!

> My idea of a perfect retirement: me, the fish, and the peace and quiet. I can fish all day if I want to. And all night, too! Yep! The big one's not going to get away this time! I'm gonna fish until I'm all fished out!

> Load up the car and paint the town red! Thanksgiving Day Sales, After-Christmas Sales, Labor Day Sales, Groundhog's Day Sales—if it's advertised, I'm there, money in hand! To think I could shop until I literally drop and then do it all again the next day! Why didn't I retire sooner?

Okay, so you're thinking about retirement! Even if these monologues are a little extreme, they're likely to cross your mind in one form or another as you contemplate the future and how you'll spend it. In our search for true fulfillment, a little fantasy sometimes gets in the way.

Retiring your old rigid schedule for the big snooze button in the sky may be a temporary pleasure, but it doesn't pass for abiding happiness. Dreaming of fishing all day may seem like heaven on earth. . .until a rainy day. . .until the fish aren't biting. Then it's back to reality. . .facing the person holding the tackle-box and figuring out what he or she is going to do to be truly happy. True happiness isn't when the fish are biting or in any person's outside circumstances. Rather, happiness is found with the person inside their circumstances.

TRUE FULFILLMENT

Fulfillment is doing things that matter. True fulfillment is deciding which things matter most and doing them first.

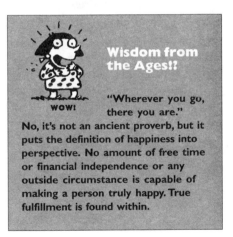

Wisdom from the Ages!!

WOW!

"Wherever you go, there you are."

No, it's not an ancient proverb, but it puts the definition of happiness into perspective. No amount of free time or financial independence or any outside circumstance is capable of making a person truly happy. True fulfillment is found within.

- Ask yourself this question:
  What three things matter most in my life?

Don't start reading again until you've truly thought about the question. Pause and read through the words above. Are you sure about your answers?

- Now ask yourself this question:
  How consistently do I give my best effort to those things?

- Now ask yourself one more question:

  What keeps me from being more consistent and giving more effort?

Your answers to the last question are keeping you from true fulfillment.

True fulfillment is about deciding what matters most in life and doing those things first. Unfortunately, we often put off what is most important to deal with the busyness of everyday life stuff.

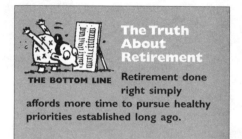

The Truth About Retirement

THE BOTTOM LINE Retirement done right simply affords more time to pursue healthy priorities established long ago.

People look forward to retirement to finally do the three things in the first question. Disappointment, however, may come when you realize a lifetime of pursuing what really didn't matter and putting off what really did is a hard habit to break. Finding true fulfillment is a lifelong journey that requires persistent work at keeping priorities all along the way.

SEARCH FOR THE HOLY GRAIL WORKSHEET

It often helps to see our deepest thoughts on paper. Grab a pen and jot down your answers to the previous questions:

QUESTION ONE
What top three things matter most to me?

1.

2.

3.

QUESTION TWO
How consistently do I give my best effort to those things?
Mark an X along this continuum that best describes your situation:

Very Consistent	Somewhat Consistent	Inconsistent
Best Effort	Moderate Effort	Little Effort

QUESTION THREE

What keeps me from being more consistent and giving more effort?

Complete these sentences if this helps you get going:

I could give more effort and time to what is most important to me if...

If only...

It would really make me happy if...

TRUE STORIES OF TRUE FULFILLMENT

You can live a life that is filled with true fulfillment. The Bible says: I have come that they may have life, and have it to the full (John 10:10). Here are a few stories of people who have lived fulfilling lives.

"I serve in our pastoral care department as part of a volunteer ministry in my church. I visit the sick and the needy and encourage the discouraged in hospitals and local nursing homes. This past winter, I was so ill I could not get out of my house. But from my home, I made over 100 calls in one month's time to wish happy birthday to members in our congregation." George Herndon, 82, Phoenix, Arizona

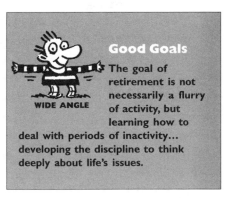

Good Goals

WIDE ANGLE

The goal of retirement is not necessarily a flurry of activity, but learning how to deal with periods of inactivity... developing the discipline to think deeply about life's issues.

"I've always dreamed of traveling when I am retired. Germany. Austria. France. England. But it seemed so selfish—all that money and nothing but photos to show for it. Instead, I'm going to travel to these same countries and more as part of the Elderhostel program.

It's an educational program for seniors with classes on all kinds of topics all over the globe. I'll have more than a slide show when I return." Annette Burns, 61, Dallas, Texas

"When I retired, I looked up our local day care center and asked if they needed volunteers at lunchtime and recess. They were delighted with my interest and asked me to visit the next day. That was five years ago. The kids I fingerpainted with that first year are now in elementary school. They still call me Papa Walters whenever we see each other. I know I made a difference in the lives of those children." Ernest Walters, 72, DeKalb, Illinois

Be Careful

THE BIBLE SAYS "Be very careful, then, how you live— not as unwise but as wise, making the most of every opportunity." (Ephesians 5:15–16)

"Having been an active person all of my life, I dreaded waking up and realizing I had nothing planned the whole day! But retirement has given me time to think about the person I am and the goals I still have for my life. I guess you could say I've become a thinker in my old age! I have time to contemplate God's Word and pray about the needs and concerns my family, friends, and I have. I feel more fulfilled as a whole person because I've learned to savor my time and not squander it." Mary Wofford, 65, New Orleans, Louisiana

THE GOALS THAT MATTER MOST

When most people think of retirement goals, their thoughts make a beeline for their wallet. While financial independence is a necessary goal to a successful retirement, it is not an end in itself. There is much more to preparing for your future than money. Some things to consider whenever you see dollar signs:

- What will you do with the money you have saved?
- Where will you be living when you spend it?
- What friends, family members, charities, etc. will share in your "wealth"?
- What activities will your money enable you to do that you couldn't do before?
- What will you do with the time you used to spend earning money?

WIDE ANGLE

Keep Perspective

Matthew 6:19–21 says, "Do not store up for yourselves treasures on earth, where moth and rust destroy, and where thieves break in and steal. But store up for yourselves treasures in heaven, where moth and rust do not destroy, and where thieves do not break in and steal. For where your treasure is, there your heart will be also."

THE ROLE OF GOALS

No matter what age you are, setting goals is crucial to living a truly fulfilling life. While it may take personal discipline to live a purpose-driven life, the benefits are very rewarding.

Bridges to the Future

"Goals are bridges that span across one's dreams to join what is to what could be." (Anonymous)

WIDE ANGLE

At retirement, one of the first battles one can face is that of depression. Up to that point, everything in life has been fairly planned with little to no effort on your part. You go to school, graduate, get a job, get married, have children and raise them, and then the process starts all over again for your kids. At retirement, the lack of structure can be intimidating and even paralyzing. Many people find they don't know what to do with their time. Having goals makes the free time your slave and not your master.

WHAT ARE MY GOALS?

A helpful exercise is to look at the dreams and goals in your life and see them on paper. We've got the paper—you supply the pen! There's something about the discipline of looking at our goals (or lack thereof) through the objectivity of pen and paper.

MY LIFE'S DREAMS

Fill in the following sections with as much detail as you can. Most sections will have more than one item listed.

Stay Sharp!

Medical science has proven inactivity and depression is linked with all kinds of illness and disease. Engaging your mind in the creation of goals and then pursuing them with passion keeps boredom at bay and may keep the doctor away, too!

WOW!

Dreams I've Already Accomplished:

Dreams I Have for My Life Now:

Dreams I Have for My Life Now: (cont)

Dreams I Have for My Future:

MY LIFE'S GOALS

Filling in this other half may show you your DREAMS page is a little too much "head in the clouds"! Goals help us to put our "feet on the ground." Go ahead and revise your DREAMS page if you have trouble coming up with corresponding realistic goals. Again, you should have more than one goal per section.

Goals I Accomplished for Dreams I've Already Achieved:

Goals I Must Have to Accomplish My Present Dreams:

Goals I Must Have to Accomplish My Present Dreams: (cont)

Goals I Have to Accomplish My Future Dreams:

GOAL-SETTING FOR THE GOAL-LESS

Admitting you need help is the first step! Many people struggle to make goals and stick to them. Getting the basics of goal-setting is the first step to a healthy, purpose-driven life—whether you are just starting your professional life or retiring from it.

Goals and Dreams

THE BOTTOM LINE

Without goals, dreams remain just that: dreams.

Look at the following acrostic to better understand the basics of Goal-setting:

G—Go for the dream!
O—Offer short-term and long-term goals
A—Act!
L—Let yourself celebrate!
S—Sit down and evaluate

GO FOR THE DREAM!

Although you'll want to be reasonable, "realistic" is something you define. Remember to factor in faith when you are dreaming of a better life.

OFFER SHORT-TERM AND LONG-TERM GOALS

Giving yourself options is a must when making goals. When we over-extend ourselves by only making long-term goals, we may tire out before we see them come to fruition.

ACT!

Don't file away your retirement goals. Put them on the fridge where you'll have to confront them each day! If one of your goals is to become closer with your family, put stationary out on your desk and write a little bit of a letter each day. When it's complete, mail it.

Work Up to It

Before you set your sights on the African jungle, you may wish to make regular involve-ment in a local

CATCH A CLUE

soup kitchen your first short-term goal. After a series of short-term service opportunities, you'll feel better prepared for the long-haul trip around the world!

LET YOURSELF CELEBRATE!

Celebrating a short or long-term goal is as important as planning for it! If one of your goals is to finish your education degree, celebrate after you pass Algebra II. If you're remodeling a room yourself, celebrate when you can walk on new carpet and not plywood—regardless of what the walls look like!

SIT DOWN AND EVALUATE

A goal is different from a dream or a desire in one major way: It's measurable. You can sit down and evaluate along the way how close you are to your objectives. Periodic review of your goals will make sure you're on the right path and not the wrong road!

GOALS! GOALS! GOALS!

Need some help jump-starting your planning? There are several areas in which to start your goal-planning. If you already have goals in many areas of your life, check out the following ideas as a chance to reevaluate or revise your standing goals.

When you retire, what goals do you have for the following areas:

• Leisure Time

• Living Location

• Marriage

- Finances

- Mental

Check Your Roots

CATCH A CLUE

Many people's fantasy retirement includes moving to an area of the country where the weather is "perfect." Before such a move, consider how you'll make new roots in your new town. Check into local chapters, churches, clubs, etc. and see how many connections you'll be able to plug into before taking up residence.

- Emotional

- Contribution to Society/Service

- Family

- Friends

- Spiritual

- Physical

LIVE FOR TODAY BUT PLAN FOR TOMORROW

EVALUATING THE IMPACT OF CHANGE

No one likes change. But the better prepared we are to face it, the better we will survive it. Retirement marks one of the greatest opportunities for change that any human being may face. For example, how will the goals you had for your marriage during your professional life be affected post-retirement? Evaluating the possibilities of change is key to a successful retirement.

EVALUATING THE "WHAT-IF'S?"

How prepared are you for change in a variety of your life's most important areas? Expecting the unexpected is great preparation for retirement.

Most of what we imagine in our retirement does not account for the unexpected. Are your goals so rigid that you have no room for flexibility? How would illness affect your long- and short-term goals?

Let's take a look at what you might do when you consider the what-if's at the time of or during your retirement. Fill in the following spaces.

What If:	I Would Be Affected in This Way:	My Plan of Action Would Be:
I or my spouse became ill or debilitated?		
I or my spouse was diagnosed with a terminal disease?		
I was widowed?		
I was divorced?		
I lost my job before retirement?		

What If:	I Would Be Affected in This Way:	My Plan of Action Would Be:
My spouse lost a job?		
My children moved back in with me?		
My parents became dependent on me?		
I have to work longer than my target date for retirement?		
My investments failed postretirement?		
I have to work part-time?		

A SPECIAL NOTE FOR SINGLE SENIOR ADULTS AT RETIREMENT

Single Senior Adults at Retirement Should Keep in Mind:

- You have more time than a married couple to spend in activities outside your home.
- You have more freedom balancing a schedule for one.
- Depression may be a special temptation. Keep your guard up against its effect.
- Some service organizations cater toward the single adult due to restricted resources. For example, it's easier to house a single adult than it is a couple in host homes in foreign countries.
- Whether you are divorced or widowed, don't face retirement alone. Get help from your lawyer and financial planners. Read books. Go to talks on retirement options. Take the initiative!
- Remain open to remarriage! People of all ages marry!

LEGACY: LIFE'S GREATER PURPOSE

Finding your life's purpose in leaving a legacy is an exciting proposition. Long after you are gone, your influence will live on in the hearts of those you touch.

Taking a simple spiritual gifts/personality inventory is a helpful tool in narrowing the field on all the areas in which you could leave a lasting contribution. Consider how the following areas of focus/giftedness best describe you as you contemplate the area in which your life's best contribution will be:

Mark your tendencies according to the following scale:

1	2	3	4
Definitely me	Sometimes me	Rarely me	Not me

Administration
___I think I am organized.
___Paperwork grabs my attention because I like it.
___I would rather solve paperwork problems than people problems.
___Potential Missions: academics, finances for small charities, senior adult council member

Encouragement

___I consider myself to be sensitive to people's needs.

___I find myself wanting to cheer up others even when I myself feel blue.

___I can motivate others through my attitude.

___Potential Missions: volunteer lay counseling at crisis pregnancy centers/youth homes, teaching in small groups

Giving/Serving

___I may not be wealthy, but I am a resourceful person.

___I am strongly motivated to help people's physical needs.

___I consider myself generous with my possessions, time, resources.

___Potential Missions: charities, Salvation Army, soup kitchens, foreign missions

Teaching

___I can communicate my thoughts and ideas clearly to groups.

___I like to research topics of interest.

___I have strong personal convictions about various issues.

___Potential Missions: Teaching courses for seniors: current events, lifestyle management, etc., Overseas opportunities in academic settings, writing

Do you see areas you might be able to serve others?

RESOURCES FOR PLANNING A FULFILLING RETIREMENT

There are a number of places you could use your talents and gifts to serve others. Here are a few:

Elderhostels—These are educational programs for seniors on national/international campuses.

Peace Corps—This organization offers service opportunities throughout the globe—long- and short-term.

Mission Boards—Many local religious denominations have mission boards with information on long- and short-term volunteer opportunities in many countries.

Church—Many local churches sponsor local, national, and international ministries for senior adults to enjoy and serve.

Retirement Communities—If your retirement community doesn't already sponsor a senior adult council, form your own! Challenge your group to adopt a local charity, day care, or youth group.

Internet—More and more computer companies are hosting internet training days for senior adults. On the Internet, you can join a number of senior citizen awareness groups for support and encouragement and travel/service opportunities.

Colleges/Universities—Many institutions have continuing education courses for active adults to complete or earn a degree in a variety of disciplines.

The Younger Generation—Volunteering at your local preschool, primary, and secondary schools would be much appreciated in many communities. Campus college groups like Campus Crusade for Christ often have lunch meetings that provide the perfect opportunity for your retirement community or church group to serve a homemade lunch to a grateful student!

SECTION 2
GETTING THERE

THE IMPORTANCE OF SAVING

BE PREPARED

Someday your work life will be done. Like everyone else, someday you'll reach that time called "retirement." It may be far in the future; it may be only a few years away. In either case, you'll need to be prepared.

Consider this: People are retiring earlier and living longer, healthier lives. You could easily spend twenty years (or one-quarter of your life) in retirement. You may get some social security, you may have a pension or retirement plan from your work, but more than likely, these will not pay you enough to be able to enjoy your current standard of living—never mind the "extras" you might be hoping to enjoy during those years.

By far the best case scenario is for you to be young and just starting in the workforce. It may seem difficult or too far away, but you should start planning even now for the day that you retire. The younger you are when you begin to save, the better off you will be at the time of retirement.

Suppose you're twenty-five years old, getting married, buying that first home, starting a family. You may feel that you can't afford to save. But you can't afford *not* to. Why? The answer is simple. The sooner you begin saving—even a small amount—the more that compound interest will work its magic on your behalf.

THE EARLIER THE BETTER

Consider the chart on the following pages. We'll take three people—Chris, Linda, and John. On the chart, you'll see that Linda invested almost three times as much money as Chris did, and for a much longer period of time. But she never accumulated as much as Chris because she waited to invest until she was forty years old. Chris, however, had begun saving at age thirty and produced over $90,000 more than Linda because the compound interest went to work for him.

Finally, look at John. He began investing at age thirty and didn't stop until he retired at age 65. He invested only $20,000 more than Linda, yet he accumulated over $230,000 more than she did because he didn't wait to start saving. That's the magic of compound interest.

Current Age	Chris	Linda	John
30	$2,000	$0	$2,000
31	2,000	0	2,000
32	2,000	0	2,000
33	2,000	0	2,000
34	2,000	0	2,000
35	2,000	0	2,000
36	2,000	0	2,000
37	2,000	0	2,000
38	2,000	0	2,000
39	2,000	0	2,000
40	0	2,000	2,000
41	0	2,000	2,000
42	0	2,000	2,000
43	0	2,000	2,000
44	0	2,000	2,000

Current Age	Chris	Linda	John
45	$0	$2,000	$2,000
46	0	2,000	2,000
47	0	2,000	2,000
48	0	2,000	2,000
49	0	2,000	2,000
50	0	2,000	2,000
51	0	2,000	2,000
52	0	2,000	2,000
53	0	2,000	2,000
54	0	2,000	2,000
55	0	2,000	2,000
56	0	2,000	2,000
57	0	2,000	2,000
58	0	2,000	2,000
59	0	2,000	2,000
60	0	2,000	2,000
61	0	2,000	2,000
62	0	2,000	2,000
63	0	2,000	2,000
64	0	2,000	2,000
65	0	2,000	2,000
Total Accumulated	**$231,439**	**$172,702**	**$404,141**
Actual Investment	($20,000)	($52,000)	($72,000)

***The above table based on 8.0% after-tax yield.*

STEP-BY-STEP

Step one, obviously, is to begin early in your life to save for your retirement days.

How much should you save? It is wise to save as much as you can. At the beginning, even if it is a few dollars, save anyway. Not only will it get you into the habit of saving, but that compound interest begins working for you. You should have a goal to save at least 10 percent of each paycheck rather than a set amount. In the chart above, those individuals would have done better by saving slightly more each year because that would have adjusted for inflation. Inflation generally creeps up 5 to 6 percent a year, so increasing saving by that much will help your savings to keep up with inflation.

Step two, then, is putting that money somewhere. But where?

A Tip About Your Uncle

CATCH A CLUE

Gone are the days when people could count on Social Security to support them during retirement. In fact, at this point, Social Security may only provide about one-third of what you'll need to live on—and it's only getting worse. (Heard all the talk recently in Washington about "saving Social Security"? That ought to send up a red flag that means we ought not count on those payments.) Social Security, even if it is "saved," cannot provide what you will need to live on in retirement. Aren't you hoping to do some special things—travel, enjoy some hobbies, visit the grandkids and do special activities with them? You won't be able to unless you've planned ahead and saved.

One big don't—DON'T keep that money in your checking account (even an interest-bearing one) or in a savings account at a bank. While compound interest still applies, the interest rates are so low that you are not getting much return. There are so many other options for investing money, and making it work and grow, that you should become informed.

The following will give you an overview of some options, and then you should consider getting financial advice from a professional who can help you weigh your options and find out what will be best for you and your family considering your age and your needs. The following descriptions are very general, and you will need to discuss with a financial planner regarding the specifics and pros and cons of each option.

401 (K)

A 401(k) may be provided through your employer which allows the employer and the employee to defer a portion of the salary to the plan. This reduces taxable income and automatically sets aside a portion of your salary into savings. In addition to employee contributions to this account, the company may make matching contributions.

These 401(k) plans provide immediate tax savings (while your salary is taxed by the government, what you put in the 401(k) is not). It is convenient because, when it's an automatic deduction, it's easier to save. You can choose, from a set of guidelines, what percentage of your paycheck you want to set aside. And, under some circumstances, these funds can be accessed before retirement if needed.

If your employer offers this, look it over, see what you're contributing, and talk to a financial advisor. Employers may also offer 403(b) plans, 457 plans, or SEPs—as well as pensions, profit sharing, etc. These all differ, so find out what your employer offers and how much you are contributing.

IRAs

Individual Retirement Accounts are just what they sound like—a place for an individual to put away money for his or her retirement. While your employer may provide a 401(k), you might also consider an IRA. This is one of the best ways to save for retirement because it is the only tax-deferred savings account that is available to everyone—even those not in the workforce or whose employers do not offer a retirement plan. *Tax-deferred* means that you pay no taxes on earnings or interest until the money in your account is withdrawn. While tax laws change, many people can still claim the contributions to their

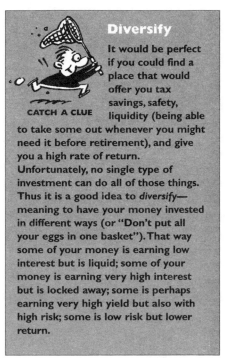

Diversify

It would be perfect if you could find a place that would offer you tax savings, safety, liquidity (being able

CATCH A CLUE

to take some out whenever you might need it before retirement), and give you a high rate of return. Unfortunately, no single type of investment can do all of those things. Thus it is a good idea to *diversify*— meaning to have your money invested in different ways (or "Don't put all your eggs in one basket"). That way some of your money is earning low interest but is liquid; some of your money is earning very high interest but is locked away; some is perhaps earning very high yield but also with high risk; some is low risk but lower return.

IRA as a tax deduction. Saving $2,000 per year in a tax-deferred IRA can provide a very important source of retirement income. Again, early contributions add up with the benefit of compound interest.

What can you put in an IRA? Think of it as a big bowl. Into that bowl you can put stocks, cash, money markets, mutual funds, etc. You can put many other types of investments into an IRA.

The hard part is that, unlike the 401(k), you need to set this money aside yourself. Thus, it is wise to get into the habit of saving and contributing to your IRA consistently in order to get the most return for your money. There is a limit to how much you can put into an IRA each year.

Roth IRA

The legislation provided by the Taxpayer Relief Act of 1997 provided for enhancements to traditional IRAs that permitted the creation of Roth IRAs. If you meet certain requirements, the money you withdraw from a Roth IRA will not be taxed (as opposed to regular IRAs which are merely tax-deferred). In other words, savings and earnings in a Roth IRA are tax-free and stay tax-free. The main difference is that the contributions to a Roth IRA are not tax deductible, as are the contributions to a traditional IRA. You can save up to $2,000 per year (or $4,000 per married couple filing jointly).

Mutual Funds

A mutual fund is an investment company that raises money from shareholders and invests in a portfolio. Every fund has specific investment objectives and policies. Mutual funds offer the benefits of diversity and professional management—as well as being available with a minimum investment. Again using the bowl analogy, think of a mutual fund as a bowl full of different kinds of stocks.

Certificates of Deposit

A certificate of deposit (CD) can be issued by banks and savings and loans. These have fixed terms and fixed rates. You invest in a CD and lock in at a certain rate. Thus, this is an excellent way to safely lock in your money at a high-interest rate when rates are falling. The downside is that they carry the risk of not being able to take advantage of higher interest rates, and there are penalties for premature liquidation.

Money Market Funds

A money market is a short-term mutual fund. This can be helpful to many investors because the money is liquid, safe, and has competitive interest rates. This is a good place to put your money if it will only be invested for a short time and if you will need to be able to access it quickly.

Stocks

Stocks are a share of ownership in a corporation. There are two main types: common and preferred. *Common stock* has a greater potential for growth and entitles shareholders to vote on matters in the company. For example, a person owning stock in a company owns a small percentage. If the corporation has 1 million shares of common stock outstanding, and you own 100 shares, then you own one ten-thousandth of the corporation. The value of your shares depends on how well the corporation performs. If it is doing well—growing and increasing in profits—then the per share value of your stock will go up. But the opposite is also true. Stocks involve risk, but have potential for very high return.

Preferred stock carries a specified dividend. It provides a fixed and high rate of dividends and is generally considered to be of higher quality than the common stock. It has a higher standing when it comes to paying dividends and receiving money back should the company have financial difficulty. There are advantages and disadvantages to preferred stock, and it would be helpful to check with a financial advisor.

The term *blue chip stocks* refers to stocks that are of national recognized, consistently profitable companies.

Bonds

A bond is a debt obligation issued by a government or corporation which promises to pay its bondholders periodic interest at a fixed or variable rate and to repay the principal after a specified period of time (called "maturity"). Bonds offer an investor the highest current cash return available, excellent liquidity, and a return of the original investment at maturity.

PLANNING FOR RETIREMENT

In planning for your retirement, you should think through several questions. You may want to obtain help from a financial advisor.

(1) What is your current income?

(2) What are your current expenses?

(3) What are your assets (home, property, money, stocks, etc.)?

(4) What are your projected expenses at retirement?

    (a) Consider all expenses as you would for making a regular budget.

    (b) In addition to basic budget needs, also consider extra funds for fun things (such as travel, hobbies, etc.)

    (c) Adjust the total of (a) and (b) at 6 percent per year for inflation. For example: If you think that you'll need $24,000 per year ($2,000 month) and it is twenty years until you retire, you will start with the $24,000 figure and multiply it by 6 percent for each year up to twenty years.

24,000 x .06 (6%) = 1,440 (+24,000 = 25,440)
25,440 x .06 = 1,526 (+ 25,440 = 26,966)
26,966 x .06 = 1,618 (+26,966 = 28,584)
etc. for a total of twenty years

In the end, you will discover that what $24,000 a year will buy today will take $76,968 (or $6,414 a month) to make the same purchases in twenty years.

(5) What income can you expect from Social Security, 401(k), or pension?

(6) Subtract your answer to number 5 (projected income) from number 4 (projected expenses). (The expenses will most often be higher than your income.) That number will tell you how much extra you will need—and how much you need to begin saving between now and then.

(7) Now subtract number 2 (current expenses) from number 1 (current income). (Hopefully, your income exceeds your expenses!) The difference is the amount of money you can save.

(8) You will want to take that savings and invest it in the best ways possible in order to make it grow into the amount that you will need in order to meet your projected expenses at retirement.

No matter what your age, you should find a professional financial planner who can help you work these numbers so you can prepare adequately for the future.

SOME COMMON MISTAKES

Too much debt—It is wise to pay off existing high-interest debts in order to be able to free up more money to save over the long term.

Keeping too much money in checking and savings accounts—While it is best to keep a small amount in a local account, the bulk of savings should be earning higher interest somewhere else

Not being able to access any money—The other extreme is to keep insufficient money in liquid accounts for emergencies. In order to meet emergencies, you need to have a sufficient reserve in a place where you can get to it if it is needed. If you don't, you will have to pull it from a place that will charge you high penalties for taking the money early.

Paying too much in income tax and not itemizing deductions—You may not feel that you have enough deductions to make itemizing worthwhile. You should attempt to itemize each year and see if it is worth it; you may be surprised. You must pay the IRS everything to which it is entitled, but you are allowed to arrange your financial affairs in order to legally reduce your tax liability. What you save from the IRS can be saved for you and your family.

Not having life insurance—Life insurance provides sufficient assets for a surviving family. If there are not enough assets and if they are not liquid, the family may have to liquidate assets at an inopportune time in order to survive. You will want to talk to a professional about what type of life insurance is best for you. You should also have adequate life insurance on a nonworking spouse (enough to replace homemaking, child care, and other activities). But you should not buy life insurance on your children—that money is better saved elsewhere.

Not having enough homeowners' insurance—You should be able to cover the replacement cost of your home and its contents. Many homeowners forget, however, that as construction costs increase over time, so does the cost of replacement. In general, replacement costs double every nine years. Make sure to update your policy so the true value of your home is covered. You would also be wise to videotape or take photographs of your home's contents and keep these in a safety deposit box. This will provide proof should a catastrophe occur.

Not having enough medical insurance—The minimum coverage individuals should have is $500,000 to $1 million, and this should be reviewed periodically.

Inadequate planning for children's education—You can assume an inflation rate of 6 percent per year, but colleges have actually raised their tuitions anywhere from 8 to 12 percent a year. For example, an 8-year-old child has ten years before entering college. If an average in-state college currently costs $9,958 per year (for tuition, fees, room and board, books, supplies, etc.); in the year 2009, that same school will cost $17,833. Remember then, to multiply that total times four, for four years. The total, adjusting for inflation, will be $78,013. You will need to plan way ahead in order to save enough for that bill when the time comes!

Inadequate planning for retirement—You should be realistic about how much money you'll need to live comfortably and plan ahead enough in order to make it possible.

Not having an estate plan and an up-to-date will—Be sure that someone in the family knows where to find all important documents.

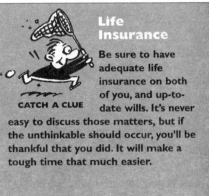

Life Insurance

Be sure to have adequate life insurance on both of you, and up-to-date wills. It's never easy to discuss those matters, but if the unthinkable should occur, you'll be thankful that you did. It will make a tough time that much easier.

CATCH A CLUE

GETTING YOUR FAMILY ON BOARD

Communication is key. Usually a quick run of the numbers will bring a big dose of reality to the spouse who doesn't worry about saving or the kids who don't understand why you won't spend, spend, spend on them.

When it comes to saving for college, show your children that you're trying to save because you have *this much* that needs to be saved in order for them to be able to go to college. Tell your children you want them to be able to attend college without the excessive strain of a full-time job or an abundance of debt afterwards. (Obviously, you will then set up a plan for them to work and save as well—and to get involved, when the time comes, in seeking out scholarships.) It is a valuable learning experience for older children to get involved with the budget so that they understand how money comes and goes, what is given, and what is saved—and why. Send them off to college understanding that hard-earned money is just that—*hard-earned*. They need to know how much things cost and the sweat it takes to earn enough money to pay the bills. They also should be learning the value of saving, even a little bit, every month.

Your spouse should always be involved in the budgeting and bill-paying process. How often it occurs that a husband suddenly passes away, leaving his wife clueless about where the bank accounts are, what bills are outstanding, where other important documents are, etc. Both husband and wife should be in communication about what's happening—even if one or the other generally handles the paperwork. There should be agreement regarding how much is going into various types of investments. Talk through your plans for the future—sending children to college as well as saving for the retirement. Be in agreement about what you'd like to do when you retire, and keep talking as the years go by. The original plan to retire to Florida may change to staying where you are. The original plan to sell the big house and get a smaller one may change to keeping that paid-off big house because so many grandkids come to visit all the time!

Talk together with a financial advisor. Communicate honestly about what you want to be able to do when you retire. Then work honestly with the numbers. Your financial advisor can help you work with various options in order to meet your goals.

SECTION 3

RETIRING EARLY

EARLY DISMISSAL?

Spend a moment thinking about it. Let the words roll off your tongue, *"Early Retirement."* The more you think about it, the more inviting it may seem:

No more deadlines
    No more unreasonable bosses
        No more irritating coworkers
            No more incompetent assistants
                No more business trips
                    No more twelve-hours shifts
                        No more *PAYCHECK!*

THAT'S the kicker now, isn't it? We might all be willing to retire early if it wasn't for this finally yet fairly significant detail.

As you fantasize about retiring early, potential activities swirl through your mind: golf, travel, missions trips, visiting family, learning a new language. All of these fantasies are nice, but can you afford to do it? Can you leave the security of a regular paycheck and begin the next exciting chapter of your life? And just because you can, should you?

IS EARLY RETIREMENT FOR YOU?

Emotionally, you might scream "YES, IT IS!" But you may need to step back and rationally look at the facts. Retirement brings significant changes.

YOU LOSE MONEY AND BENEFITS

- Can you afford to live without your paycheck? Do you have enough money in savings? Do you have or need another source of income? Will your IRA, pensions, or other retirement benefits be penalized if you draw on them early? Is the debt you have manageable with your projected retirement income?
- Can you replace or live without the other benefits you receive from your work? Let's go beyond your paycheck. What other benefits do you depend on? Health insurance? Company car? Club memberships? Travel expenses? Education reimbursements?
- Can you replace your health coverage? Unless you're in an unusual financial position, you shouldn't live without health insurance. Even if you're in shape and feel great, an unsuspected accident or undetected illness can cost you thousands, ten thousands—or a lot more.

You might decide you can live without the paycheck. Double-check that. It can be harder to get rehired than to stay hired. (If you do get rehired, it probably won't be at the same pay scale.) You may have enough to live, but do you have enough to cover the special situations you may encounter? Is anyone depending on you for support? Do you have aging parents, college-bound children, or a child about to be a married child?

YOUR FAMILY LIFE CHANGES

- What does your job mean to your social and family life? You may not have thought much about this aspect of your work before, but it might be your primary locale of friendships. What will replace that interaction? How will your family react to the change? When will your spouse retire?

What will your family do with you? They probably won't appreciate it if you rearrange the garage each week. They may go crazy if you're idly around the house poking your nose into things you haven't poked your nose into for twenty-five years.

THE SATISFACTION OF A JOB WELL DONE

- What satisfaction does your job give to you? If you depend on your job for certain fulfillment, what will you do when it's gone? Do you love solving problems at work? What will you do to find that fulfillment elsewhere? Remember, your spouse might not appreciate you jumping in "to solve" a whole new set of household problems.

Ultimately, golf is not fulfilling. It's fun and enjoyable, and you might look forward to spending more time on the links, but you need something else to do. It's very important to stay busy with something you find fulfilling. It doesn't need to be something that pays well, but that gives your day-to-day work meaning.

HOW TO GET THERE

You don't have to have a six-figure job to save enough for retirement. You've probably heard stories about unlikely millionaires—bus drivers, city workers, teachers, assembly line workers. Being able to afford retirement—and early retirement—doesn't take a huge paycheck but it does take a few disciplines.

WIDE ANGLE

Early Benefits

Many people retire early. According to a survey from Merrill Lynch, 76 million baby boomers plan on retiring before they turn sixty-five. You can take many retirement benefits early—but there may be penalties.

For example, your Social Security benefits can be taken a few years early but with penalty. In fact, over 70 percent of retirees take their first social security check early. Since the requirements and laws change frequently, you should speak to your financial planner directly about this option.

1. Save now. It's never too early to start.

That advice is of little help to you if you're already nearing retirement age. But if you have some years ahead of you, use them well. See the chart in "Getting There" that shows that advantage of saving early. If you've already missed the chance at starting young, pass this information on to your children, young coworkers, or your friends' children. No matter your age, you should save toward your retirement.

The key to being successful is to create a regular plan and stick to it. This is most easily accomplished by participating in a company 401(k) plan where your money is withdrawn directly from your check. If your company doesn't have such a plan, create your own. Meet with a financial planner or set up your own mutual fund retirement account. Save as much as you can. You'll need a large nest egg so you can live off enough interest to pay you 60–90 percent of your preretirement income.

2. If possible, save tax-deferred.

401(k) plans allow you to withdraw pre-tax dollars from your paycheck. That means money is siphoned away to your retirement account *before* Uncle Sam gets his share of it. Many companies will match the money you put into retirement. That means if you put 2 percent of your salary away, they'll put 2 percent more—that's *free* money. Take them up on it!

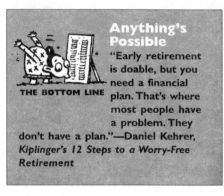

Anything's Possible

"Early retirement is doable, but you need a financial plan. That's where most people have a problem. They don't have a plan."—Daniel Kehrer, *Kiplinger's 12 Steps to a Worry-Free Retirement*

THE BOTTOM LINE

3. Open an IRA.

This step is best after you've maxed out your 401K plan (or if your company doesn't have one). It might also be a good place to diversify if your company plan isn't diversified. Traditional IRAs are better than regular investment or savings account because the money grows tax-free until you withdraw it. Of course, there's a 10 percent penalty if you withdraw the money early, so be sure you're socking away money you intend to retire on.

4. Be diversified.

You don't want all your retirement money in one area of the stock market or in any other one thing (including your house). There's no set formula for where you want your money because some people have more stomach for risk than others. Visit www.quicken.com for help deciding what kind of retirement portfolio is best for you.

QUESTIONS AND ANSWERS

HOW MUCH DO YOU NEED TO RETIRE?

Probably more than you think.

Most financial experts say you need a nest egg that will give you 60–80 percent of your preretirement income. If you were living well below your means, you could get by with less. If you were always maxing out your budget, you should probably have more.

Plan on having your retirement income last a long time. The current, average life expectancy is about eighty years. But you'd probably be wise to plan on living to be 100. You'd like to live that long, wouldn't you?

WHAT'S A GOOD GOAL FOR YOUR NEST EGG?

Here's a hypothetical situation that you can consider but it probably won't apply directly to you. Every budget and every need is different. There are a lot of factors to keep in mind while making your decision (health, budget, mortgages, cost of living increases, etc). (Note: This chart assumes you will not receive any Social Security benefits.)

Person: A married couple who makes $75,000 a year

Desired income after retirement $45,000 a year
between the ages of 65–100
(plus 3 percent a year increase for inflation).

Pensions and social security receivable: None

Be a Better Saver

THE BOTTOM LINE Here's some practical ideas to increase your retirement nest egg and decrease your yearly expenses.

- Invest in a 401(k) plan. You save on taxes and the money is tax-deferred. Some employers will match your contribution.
- Save early and often. Start as young as you can and save at least 10–15 percent of your income. This will never be easy later. Find ways to do it.
- Pass on "nice to have" things that you don't need (an exotic vacation, a new living room set, a spiffy new computer). Save the money instead.
- Never carry a balance on your credit card. It almost never makes sense to pay credit card interest. Why make Visa richer and you poorer?
- Trim your cost of living. Look for ways to spend less. Buy economy items when you can. Buy a used car. Move to a smaller house. Refinance your mortgage.
- Know your expenses. Are you paying more on your phone bill for features you don't use?
- Refigure your insurance. Many people carry too much coverage on their car. Are you carrying collision insurance on an old car? When was the last time you got a new bid on your term life insurance? Answering these questions can save you hundreds of dollars a year
- Take less expensive vacations. Drive rather than fly.

| Amount needed: | At least $500,000–$650,000 with at least 9 percent annual return |

This chart is for illustration use only. Please discuss your situation with a certified financial planner.

WILL SOCIAL SECURITY BE AROUND TO HELP YOU?

For those approaching retirement age, probably. For those with retirement in the distant future, we don't know. Sure, we'd like to believe that all the money we've been pumping into the system will be there for us, but the government will probably overhaul the system in some way. Until we see what they do, it's best to plan on not receiving any social security money. Make your retirement plan work without it. If it's there for you, you'll be better off.

SECTION 4
HELP! MY SPOUSE RETIRED!!

HOW YOUR SPOUSE'S RETIREMENT AFFECTS YOU

You prepare for a new puppy.
You prepare for a wedding.
You prepare for having kids.
You prepare for the kids to leave.
You prepare for retirement...or do you?

For you, does preparing for retirement mean mutual funds and pension plans? Have you prepared for suddenly facing unlimited time with your spouse and the structural changes that will produce in your marriage? Have you prepared for the change in expectations as roles and rules are thrown to the wind? Have you prepared for how you are going to maintain the privacy YOU need as both of you change your lives?

Yikes! This is a big deal—something to be prepared for, even practiced at, not just drifted into with no forethought or planning.

Most of a married couple's adult life is scheduled and ordered by kids and work. Usually by retirement time the kids are grown and somewhat out of the picture, or at least out of the house. Work, then, takes a backseat and suddenly two people face the unfamiliar situation of having unlimited amounts of time together.

Once again—yikes!

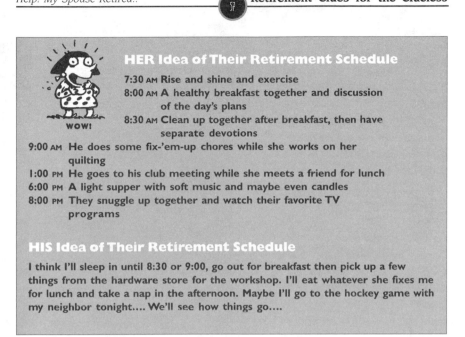

HER Idea of Their Retirement Schedule

7:30 AM Rise and shine and exercise
8:00 AM A healthy breakfast together and discussion of the day's plans
8:30 AM Clean up together after breakfast, then have separate devotions
9:00 AM He does some fix-'em-up chores while she works on her quilting
1:00 PM He goes to his club meeting while she meets a friend for lunch
6:00 PM A light supper with soft music and maybe even candles
8:00 PM They snuggle up together and watch their favorite TV programs

HIS Idea of Their Retirement Schedule

I think I'll sleep in until 8:30 or 9:00, go out for breakfast then pick up a few things from the hardware store for the workshop. I'll eat whatever she fixes me for lunch and take a nap in the afternoon. Maybe I'll go to the hockey game with my neighbor tonight.... We'll see how things go....

WHAT MIGHT HAPPEN

The most common scenario involves a husband who steps away from full-time employment and is suddenly involved in what used to be solely his wife's territory—the home. The very fact that he is home more means that he is more involved in what happens at home instead of hearing about it when he calls. This can create shock waves in a relationship that has often worked a certain way for a long time.

The first thing that most wives complain about when their husbands retire is lunch. Suddenly he's home for lunch. Can she still keep lunch dates? Is she responsible for cooking yet another meal? If he makes his own lunch is she prepared to deal with this intrusion into the system of her kitchen? ("Hon, I'm just asking, why does ANYONE need six cans of tuna?") Lunch itself is not the big deal, but the changed system is.

Another common complaint is the fact that a wife can't seem to have a conversation on the phone without a husband chiming in. ("It was the thirteenth, not the fourteenth and we were at the Bronsons!") While this is surely a common occurrence (no wife, of course, ever chimed in on her husband's conversation), the issues are about privacy and change and making your marriage stretch into a different shape, but still work.

So, yes, if your spouse retires it is going to affect you. The best preparation is awareness and communication.

GETTING ALONG. . .AGAIN

So what can husbands and wives do to make the most of their retirement years together?

Spending Time Together Before

WIDE ANGLE

Which statement most accurately describes the kind of time you spent with your spouse before retirement?

1. We spent most weekday evenings and weekends in each other's company.
2. We passed in the hall during the week, but on weekends we enjoyed each other's company quite a bit.
3. We passed in the hall during the week and saw each other on the weekends, but usually in the presence of other people.
4. We were on very different schedules all the time.

First of all, PREPARE for them! Talk about expectations, hopes, and dreams. Is he hoping to be together all the time? Is she worried about giving up her lunches with girlfriends? Talk about schedules and roles. Does he WANT to start sharing in the meal preparation? Does she feel comfortable giving up what was formerly her territory?

ROLE MODELS

Begin to look for role models. Watch older couples and get to know them. Find out what has worked for them and hopefully avoid some pitfalls that they faced and survived.

Spending Time Together After

THE BOTTOM LINE Which statement most accurately describes the kind of time you would like to spend together after retirement?

1. I'd like for us to spend most of our time together.
2. I'd like for us to pursue different interests but still spend time together every day.
3. I'd like for us to pursue different interests but socialize together.
4. I'm dreading the time we spend together.

Next, PRACTICE this new way of living. Even before retirement, go ahead and let him start preparing dinner or doing some grocery shopping (horrors!). If he's looking forward to more time to play golf together, start playing more now. If she's been wanting to grow a garden, start this year instead of waiting for next. Let some of the changes begin so that the changes of retirement are not quite so sudden and "cold turkey."

Also, understand what kind of privacy each of you will need. It's better to talk about it now than when there are hurt feelings because you have different expectations. Sudden unlimited time together is really not such a carefree thing. Each person in a couple must decide how much is enough and how much is too much. Then, get ready to find a way to communicate about that so that neither feels unwanted.

Above all, keep your sense of humor. If you are suddenly going to be thrown headlong into each other's faces, you had better be able to laugh at what you see in front of you—especially when you look in the mirror. You will get on each other's nerves more if you are together more. It's the nature of humans within four walls. Better to laugh than to cry or scream or walk out or be miserable.

Some Rules for the Road...

- A wife is not responsible for her husband's boredom.
- A husband is not responsible for his wife's happiness.
- A wife is not the sole owner of the kitchen utensils.
- A husband does not get to make any size mess while he's cooking with no thought about cleaning it up.

DON'T FORGET

BE FLEXIBLE

Allow the structure of the marriage to change but talk about it every step of the way. If she has been used to having ladies over for bridge or Bible study, talk with him beforehand about whether he should join in or find something else to do. Keep saying to yourself over and over, "Different can be better. It never hurts to try something new."

How closely does your before-retirement description match your after-retirement hopes? If you're hoping for a big change, then it's going to take some work to make it happen. Start talking about it now.

CATCH A CLUE

Mistaken Identities

- *"I hired a contractor on the sly to convert our shed into a workshop for my husband. He always said that when he retired he was going to have all the time he wanted to putter and he couldn't wait. He wasn't excited though when he saw the renovated workshop. He seemed disappointed and I felt hurt."*

At one time her husband did want a workshop, but the last few years at the job had taken its toll. Now, he really wanted to just relax and spend time with his wife. This workshop just made him feel like she was getting him out of her hair.

- *"I know my wife loves to go and do, so we've joined every club and bowling league we could find. We dance, we create, we bowl, we play games. Our weeks are full of activities we do together. Yet, we don't seem any closer."*

His wife has always involved herself in a lot of activity because he was never home. Now that he has a more flexible schedule, she'd like to make up for some of that lost time by spending time with just the two of them and getting to know each other. She wonders why he never seems to want to be alone with her.

- *"I am so sick of going to the same beach cottage every year. There are so many places to see; why does my husband insist on coming to this same shack? I just try and make the best of it."*

He feels the same way. He's tired of the beach but she goes on and on about their memories there so he keeps making the reservation.

The moral of these stories? It never hurts to check in and see what matters to each other...not just once, but every so often.

BEING INVOLVED IN THE DECISIONS

While both spouses are working, marriages are often weekend affairs. During the week the evenings are taken up in household chores or vegging in front of the TV. So retirement will be like a Saturday night, every night right? No, that's not the way it works. Everybody's life has to come down to some kind of schedule no matter how free or flexible their spirit may be. Once you retire, the things that drove that schedule change. There are more choices. In some ways that makes life easier, but in other ways it makes it more difficult.

The important thing is to make those choices together. You won't be doing your marriage a favor by deferring constantly to your spouse. Retirement is about both of your dreams. As difficult as it may be at times, you need to talk about those dreams from the broad strokes to the details. You need to look out for each other and for yourself in terms of that balance of togetherness as well as privacy in your day-to-day schedule. This, in turn, will lay a good foundation for talking about the big dreams—like where you will live and when you will get there and who wants to start a business on the side, etc.

In reality, you aren't just retiring FROM jobs or a familiar life. You are retiring TO a new venture. Part of the venture is this relationship that you have maintained already through many phases of life will now face yet one more.

KEEPING LOVE ALIVE

The great lesson of retirement: Life is not what you did, but what you are doing. It's not what kids you raised and things you accomplished, it's what you are doing now. Your marriage is the same marriage, it just changes shape according to what you ask from it.

The truth about relationships, including marriage, is that they rarely stay the same. Instead they either get better or worse. And certainly they cannot stay the same through a life-changing event like retirement. So you can choose to let this change either revitalize your marriage or intensify what is already bad.

Maybe you've been distant. Maybe you've been busy. But there's hardly a woman that won't warm up to a man who wants to be with her because he's crazy about her. And there's hardly a man who won't do anything for a woman who openly adores him. Give each other space, but nurture your love for each other.

More research is revealed every day that sexually, emotionally, and physically you can enjoy each other for many years to come. Don't waste a minute.

HIS GREAT EXPECTATIONS QUIZ

His Questions
Circle or fill in the response that most accurately describes your expectations and wishes. Afterwards compare answers and start talking.

1. Do you expect your wife to spend her daytime hours with you now that you are retired?   Yes   No

2. Should your wife tell you if she has plans to go out on the next day?   Yes   No

3. Would you mind your wife's entertaining women friends at home while you are there?   Yes   No

4. Do you see the kitchen as your wife's domain?   Yes   No

5. Do you expect to share more of the household chores after you are retired?   Yes   No

6. Would you like your wife to participate more with you in your hobbies?
   Yes   No

7. Circle the activities that you'd like to do more of with your wife:

   Go to the movies   Go to professional ball games   Go to the ballet

   Go sightseeing   Take day trips   Play sports together

   Go fishing   Take continuing ed. courses

   Other _____

8. Do you hope to make love more after you are retired? Yes   No

9. How often do you enjoy going out with friends to dinner?
   _____ nights/week   month

10. How often do you enjoy going out to dinner with only your spouse?
    _____ nights/week   month

HER GREAT EXPECTATIONS QUIZ

Her Questions

Circle or fill in the response that most accurately describes your expectations and wishes. Afterwards compare answers and start talking.

1. Do you expect to spend your daytime hours with your husband now that he is retired?   Yes   No

2. Should you have to tell your husband if you have plans to go out on the next day?   Yes   No

3. Would you entertain women friends at home while he is there?
   Yes   No

4. Do you see the kitchen as your domain?   Yes   No

5. Do you expect him to share more of the household chores after he is retired?   Yes   No

6. Would you like to participate more with your husband in his hobbies?
   Yes   No

7. Circle the activities that you'd like to do more of with your husband:

   Go to the movies   Go to professional ball games   Go to the ballet

   Go sightseeing   Take day trips   Play sports together

   Go fishing   Take continuing ed. courses

   Other _____

8. Do you hope to make love more after you are retired? Yes   No

9. How often do you enjoy going out with friends to dinner?
   _____ nights/week   month

10. How often do you enjoy going to dinner with only your spouse?
    _____ nights/week   month

SECTION 5
HOW TO ENJOY YOUR RETIREMENT

ENJOY YOUR RETIREMENT

Whether you have prepared well for retirement or prepared at all, the fact remains that life is ever passing by and it's important that you breathe deeply and enjoy the moments given you. As you face retirement more of your life lies behind than ahead. It is more important to invest in the quality of your life than ever before.

Think about what makes you happy:
- the activities you enjoy
- the new experiences you want to have
- the people you hold dear
- the places you love
- the reflection you owe yourself
- the recreation you need

Think about what makes your life feel full or meaningful:
- the people you help
- the love you feel
- the safety of your surroundings
- the contribution you can make
- the sum total of what you have to offer and receive

All these things enter into the equation that totals enjoying your own retirement. Retirement is no different than the rest of your life in the sense that it's up to you to figure out what will make you happy and then do it. It all has to do with making choices and then preparing to act on those choices. Too often retirees feel their choices have been diminished rather than broadened. They may be reminded too often that they are living on a *fixed* income, that they aren't spring chickens anymore, that technology is passing them by. Instead they need to remind themselves that they are now smart enough to really make the most of life and their time will be free enough to do just that.

When retirees are asked what enables them to enjoy their retirement, "preparation" is the number one answer. That preparation includes being prepared financially but also being prepared emotional and socially. It includes knowing what you want and what your spouse wants and then making sure you have a way to get those things.

IS IT OKAY TO SPEND WHAT YOU'VE SAVED?

Well, not the first day. But it's a good question to ask. You spend years getting ready for retirement, setting up savings plans, 401(k)s, etc., then suddenly you retire and you're supposed to move from the "saving for a rainy day" mode into the "dipping into the kitty" mode. Can you do without guilt? Yes! You can and you should.

LONG-TERM GOALS

Now, that's not to say that you should lose sight of your long-term goals. (You could see that one coming, couldn't you?) You probably know what your basic monthly bills will be. But you need to be just as aware of what you

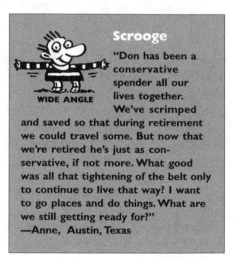

WIDE ANGLE

Scrooge

"Don has been a conservative spender all our lives together. We've scrimped and saved so that during retirement we could travel some. But now that we're retired he's just as conservative, if not more. What good was all that tightening of the belt only to continue to live that way? I want to go places and do things. What are we still getting ready for?"
—**Anne, Austin, Texas**

and your spouse would like to accomplish with your retirement in terms of travel and enjoyment as well as savings and money management.

There are as many ways to structure your retirement spending as there are to structure your retirement savings. And for many, it is just as scary. First you need to have firmly in your mind what parts of your income are

fixed and unchangeable. Your pension check is a good example. It's going to be the same every month. But you will also have income-producing assets like savings accounts, securities, and investments. You'll need to ask yourself questions such as:

CATCH A CLUE

A Little Help

"We always dread meeting with our accountant. We've never been really good with money. I'm surprised we have any savings at all. We do keep a tight rein on our spending when we're at home, though, clipping coupons and watching the sales papers. I'll tell you why. It's because we are committed to taking some trips we've always wanted to take. It's worth facing the accountant and his pencil if it means we'll see Alaska this year and take the kids to Nova Scotia the next."
—**Deloris, Quebec**

1. Are my income-producing assets earning as much interest as they should?

2. Should I switch from one kind of asset to another (from checking to savings, from savings to CDs)?

3. Are there ways we can cut our daily living expenses that we might not even miss?

4. Can our monthly credit payments be reduced by selling something or consolidating bills at a lower interest rate?

5. Can we keep better records of our expenses so that our taxes are less?

If financial matters are daunting to you, you might inquire at some of these organizations for information or guidance about managing your retirement assets once you are already retired:

- AFL-CIO Community Services Department
- AARP Worker Equity Department
- American Bankers Association
- Consumer Information Center
- Council of Better Business Bureaus
- Credit Union National Association
- Federal Trade Commission
- Money Management Institute
- National Consumers League
- National Institute of Age, Work, and Retirement
- Pension Rights Center
- Service Corps of Retired Executives (SCORE)
- Small Business Administration
- United Senior Health Cooperative
- US Department of Labor

DON'T FORGET

Buyer Beware!

No matter what stage of life you are in, it can look very inviting to make money fast. Be wary if any schemes presented to you have these traits:
- You are asked to make a check out to an individual rather than a company.
- You are discouraged from calling references or asking for a second opinion.
- You are asked to grant power of attorney to your salesman or advisor.
- You are asked to pay a timing fee for an alert on an investment.
- You are put under great pressure to respond quickly.
- You are promised results that seem too good to be true.
- You are promised a risk-free investment.
- You are refused information in writing.

So the answer to the question is, "Yes, Virginia, you can spend what you saved for retirement." Just spend it wisely so that you can enjoy it for as long as possible. You've worked hard to get there. You've spent a lifetime saving and planning for this ticket called retirement. Enjoy the ride just as much as you can.

ACTIVITIES: THE ANSWER TO THE "WHAT WILL I DO?" QUESTION

For most retirees who are in good health boredom is not an issue. In fact, more often than not you hear questions like, "How did I ever have time to work?" or "What did I do before and how did I have time to do it?"

Because of the size of the current generation in retirement and the current generation preparing for retirement, activities abound. What do you like to do?

- Play social games?
- Play sports?
- Learn new skills?
- Meet new people?
- Read new books?

Strike or Spare?

"The first time I dragged my wife out to a bowling league you would have thought we were going to the hospital for the worst procedure available. She was bound and determined to hate every minute of it. You ought to see her now. She's rushing ME out the door. She's made some real friends on the league. It's nice that we have something we can do together. Even nicer for her that she beats my score half the time!"
—Neal, Covington, Louisiana

- Go new places?
- Volunteer where you're needed?

Whatever you enjoy, there is probably an activity that will match in your city or a city nearby. Check your weekend listings in the paper. Walk slowly by bulletin boards. Keep an eye out for senior activity newsletters.

Here is just a sampling of the kinds of activities that go on all the time just waiting for you to become involved.

Juniors and Seniors

"There's this community center pretty close to our neighborhood.

WOW!

Before we retired we figured it was mainly for kids to play ball and get into trouble. Now that we've had time to check it out though, there are a lot of things for us to do there. We often go out to dinner, then walk around the track before my wife goes to her ceramics class and I play cards with some friends. Who would have thought that I'd be enjoying the same place where teenagers play pick-up games and little old ladies (don't tell her I said that) do crafts?"
—Jim, Danbury, Connecticut

Classes

    Cooking
    Computer
    Music (singing, playing)
    Foreign language
    Lifelong Learning institutes
    Correspondence classes

Clubs

    Book clubs
    Dinner clubs
    Garden clubs
    Travel clubs

Crafts

    Ceramics

Pottery
Leatherworking
Woodworking
Tole painting

Faux finish painting

Community theatre

Community band or orchestra

Games

Bingo
Keeno
Rook
Bridge
Pinochle

Dancing

Contra dancing
Square dancing
Line dancing
Ballroom dancing
Country Western (Kicker) dancing

Exercise

Walking
Low-impact aerobics
Swimming
Weight lifting

Travel

Group tours
Day trips
Bed & Breakfasts
Mini-cruises
Weekend shopping trips

DON'T FORGET

Basic Travel Tips

- Travel in the "off" season for less expense and hassle.
- Sign up for frequent flyer miles.
- Check into senior deals where you pay one price and fly several times throughout the year anywhere in the country.
- Read the fine print before you sign anything, including a check to a travel agent.
- Start as early as possible and keep asking about better prices or possible deals that might take just a little more "hunting."
- Consider travelling with a group. Your schedule won't be as much your own, but a lot of the work will be done for you.
- Travel light. You really can do without the whole closet. Pack what you want to take, then try to cut it by half.
- Always ask if there is an 800 number available for hotels rather than use a toll number.
- Use public transportation when you are in a new place so you are free to look around.
- Check out travel discounts available to you through organizations you may already be a member of like AARP, AAA, occupational professional organizations, and travel clubs.
- Check into traveler's health insurance.
- Don't carry more cash than is necessary.
- Don't hesitate to ask for help or directions.
- Don't take anything you couldn't bear to lose.

Sports

- Bowling
- Fishing
- Golf classes and tournaments, as well as driving ranges
- Cross-country skiing

Volunteering

- Homeless centers
- Libraries
- Church
- Elementary schools

Working part-time

- Consignment stores
- Antique stores or malls
- Retail stores
- Home repair
- Starting your own business

TAKING VACATIONS

Any travel agent will tell you, the way to really enjoy a vacation is to prepare for it. You don't have to prepare like you would before you take your SATs, but you do need to

CATCH A CLUE

Vacate!

"We've never been much for vacations. We always ended up going to see my sister or his parents. Then we used our vacation weeks to see the kids and grandkids. So, really, I never expected to do a lot of vacationing once we were retired. But, you know, we really enjoy it. Don't get me wrong; we don't go climb mountains or anything. In fact, if we can we stay with the same hotel chain everywhere we go. Still, we have seen a lot of cities that we never dreamed of seeing. And we're getting pretty good at sniffing out the best little collectibles shops. We often say to ourselves that we should have started vacationing much earlier in our lives, but, the truth is there was never the time. We were always rushing some-where. I think we enjoy it so much now because we really can stroll through the places we go."
—Gladys, Gainsville, Florida

do a little research. Why? Because if you don't, you'll spend your time on vacation trying to figure out what to do each day. At least read brochures ahead of time and compare interests with your travel companion. If you already know the highlights you don't want to miss, then you can structure your "wander" time around those events.

For information about a city you'll be vacationing in, call information for the number of the Chamber of Commerce and request information or call your local travel agencies. Generally any city is glad to send you information so that you will come and spend your tourism dollars there.

Popular Vacation Activities

- Go on a bird-watching trip.
- Visit architectural centers.
- Attend theatre productions.
- Take a trip to your past.... Look up ancestors, visit places your husband saw in the war, find the places where your grandparents lived, go back to where you spent your teenage years, visit your colleges....
- Take a cruise on a liner or even charter your own boat.
- Sign up for a preplanned package tour.
- Take a train ride.
- Invest in a time-share.
- Go camping either in a tent or a cabin.

WIDE ANGLE

Ever heard of Vacation Deficit Disorder?

It's what happens when you work, work, work until you think you cannot work anymore. It's what happens to those people who let their sick days and vacation days pile up until the boss says, "Use it, or lose it." It's what makes people yearn for retirement but then be miserable two weeks afterwards. Why? Because what they really wanted was a vacation. Remember to take time off. Use your vacation time to explore places that you may want to visit for longer periods after you retire (or even live there).

Don't be a victim of Vacation Deficit Disorder!

- Take a soft adventure tour (active, but low impact).
- Take part in an International Homestay (host families in other countries allow you to share their home and culture).
- Join a travel club.
- Go to a theme or amusement park.
- Pick a city and explore.
- Meet old friends in a city none of you have visited before.
- Explore a national park.
- Visit a dude ranch.
- Go on a photo safari.
- Take a hot-air balloon ride.
- Take one grandchild at a time on a special trip.
- Rent an RV and take a road trip.
- Visit a tropical island.
- Visit every state you've never been to.

WOW!

Memories

"Our friends, Lisa and Royce, moved away when their kids were in high school. We've kept in touch at Christmas and birthdays, but we didn't expect to really see each other again. Once we were all retired, though, we took a short vacation together to Atlanta. We went to a Braves' game and ate out every night. It was so much fun. Since then we've vacationed together a couple of times a year. We've even talked about picking out a retirement village to move to so that as we get less able to travel we can still spend time together.

We sure are making some good memories together. Who would have thought, after all these years?"
—Danelle, Houston, Texas

Popular Vacation Places in the U.S.
- Grand Canyon
- Jackson Hole, Montana
- Charleston, South Carolina
- St. Augustine, Florida
- Kalispell, Montana
- Las Vegas, Nevada

- San Diego, California
- San Antonio, Texas
- Hershey, Pennsylvania
- Yosemite National Park, California
- Walt Disney World, Florida
- Sea World
- Disneyland, California
- The Everglades, Florida
- Savannah, Georgia
- Washington, D.C.
- Door County, Wisconsin
- Alaska
- Hawaii

Group Travel

Taking group tours is one of the most economical ways to travel. Usually you book a reservation for these tours through a travel agent. Here are some very important questions to ask so that you don't face too many unwelcome surprises.

Here's a Cruise Tip...

Be sure your room isn't near the engine room, the galley, or the dance hall to cut down on heat and noise.

CATCH A CLUE

- Is the tour price "all-inclusive"? (Sometimes the price is land arrangements only and airfare is separate.)
- What extras will be charged?
- Which areas will we "visit" and which will we only "drive through"?
- How much walking is involved each day?

- How much freetime is included for shopping or exploring or resting?
- How many meals per day are included in the package?
- What is the baggage allowance?
- What is the length of a typical day from "have to get up" to "finally get to go to bed"?

Consider Elderhostel

Elderhostel is an educational travel program for people sixty years and older. It is similar to an educationally themed tour. You will often stay in dorm-type rooms and eat cafeteria style, but the cost will be modest and you will see more of the "real" face of the country rather than the tourist or commercial face. The fees often cover all costs except transportation and any side excursions that you plan yourself. There are instructors and there are field trips but there are no exams or homework. Sometimes your trip even includes a stay with a local family. For more information about Elderhostel, call 877-426-8056.

World Travel

"I always get a little nervous going through customs. We've been out of the country several times so I'm used to it and I always know our passports are up to date, but still I just breathe easier when we know the bags are cleared and we're on our way. I never would have believed that at my age I would become a world traveler, but I guess I am."
—Ellis, Jamul, California

WOW!

TRAVELING ABROAD

Your Passport

Start working on your passport three months before you plan on crossing the border. You'll need to apply in person to a local passport agency. They'll need your birth certificate and other proof of identification. They'll also need passport photos which you can usually have taken at quick-print shops. Passports are usually valid for ten years. Often you can renew them by mail. Always check your renewal date BEFORE you are on the way to the airport. Go ahead and make a photocopy of your passport so that you'll have the information if you need to replace your passport. Keep the copy in a separate place from your passport, perhaps with your spouse.

Your Visa

You need a passport before you can apply for a visa. A visa is a stamp that represents your permission to enter a country for a specific amount of time and purpose. Visas usually take several weeks to clear.

THE BOTTOM LINE

Just Like Shopping

"I remember the first time we crossed the border. We were going to spend five days in Costa Rica. As we showed our passports I felt such a thrill. But then as we began to hear less English I got a little nervous. What if we couldn't find our way around? What if we needed help and couldn't tell anyone?

"Those fears are all behind us now. We zip in and out of countries like we used to zip in and out of the grocery store. It just takes doing it a few times. And you know what? I have found friendly, helpful people across every border I have traveled. It's been a great retirement so far."
—Katharine, Silver Cliff, Colorado

Your Immunizations

Yes, depending on where you are going, you may need to get some "shots." Sometimes a country requires these shots to protect you. Other times the shots protect the citizens of that nation from YOUR germs. Interesting thought, huh? Some of the typical immunizations are:

- Yellow Fever
- Cholera
- Polio
- Rubella
- Tetanus
- Measles
- Whooping cough

If you don't know what immunizations you need, you can often receive this kind of information from the State Department in Washington D.C. or the U.S. Public Health Service. Your doctor may have the necessary information as well.

Tips for Travelling Abroad

- Don't pack your passport in your luggage. Keep it with you.
- Most foreign countries have tourist offices in New York City—call ahead for brochures and travel information
- Take a phrase book. It at least shows an effort on your part.
- Duty-free doesn't mean discount—in any language.
- Don't assume pay phones work the same in every country.
- Ask about the tipping customs before you hand over money that is not expected.
- Don't skip meals. You're using more energy than you realize in a strange place, no matter how much fun you're having.
- Carry a collapsible bag in your suitcase to carry souvenirs home.
- If you are going to be in a country other than your own for more than a month, check in with the U.S. consulate there when you arrive. Should you run into any trouble, this short visit may stand you in good stead.
- Reconfirm your flights at each stopover. Some foreign airlines don't recognize your reservation unless you have reconfirmed it at the gate or the ticket counter.

Popular Vacation Spots Abroad
- Aztec Ruins
- Brazilian Rain Forest
- Canada—every part
- Cancun, Mexico
- Costa Rica
- Greek Islands
- Guadalajara, Mexico
- Ireland
- London, England
- Paris, France
- Scotland

Travel Insurance—a Must

Before you head out for any long trips, give some thought to travel insurance. You can purchase insurance for different amounts, but a typical policy might cover up to $10,000 for foreign hospital and physician fees plus the cost to get you back to your home or a familiar facility. Most travel agents can steer you to an insurance company that carries this type of insurance, or you can call your own insurance company and make some inquiries. Often you can just add on to your current health insurance policy for the time of your travel.

GIVING BACK TO OTHERS

WIDE ANGLE

Give Back

"I remember when I was a young woman and my aunts started giving away all their dishes and collectibles. I was happy to have something of theirs but I couldn't believe they would part with such memories. Now that I'm retired I understand what they were thinking. I don't need all these things. I'd much rather give them to someone who matters to me, someone who will think of me when they use them, someone who is still accumulating their household. Besides, I'm too busy now that Ned and I are both retired to keep up with all this stuff. It's time to pass some things on, to give some things back."
—Bonnie, Springfield, Illinois

Take a moment to think back to your life as a teenager or young adult. Let your mind wander through the people in your life that were "old" or "retired" then. How did they look to you? What did they offer? What role did they play in your life?

If you're like most, those people seemed to have it together, to be stable, to be exactly where they wanted to be. Now, you are anticipating being one of those people. It probably doesn't seem as surefooted a journey and in some ways, given the changing decades, it probably isn't. What did those retired adults offer to you? What kind of role models were they? What kind of role model will you be?

There are many people who have supported you through your journey to retirement. Use part of your retirement as a time to give back to those people. A good place to start is with your wife and kids.

SPENDING MORE TIME WITH YOUR SPOUSE

You wait all your working life to retire and be together—then it happens. Suddenly you are face-to-face with a person that you may have never had unlimited time with. It's a change. It's a new phase. It's…a little unnerving.

As you prepare for retirement, take some short trips together. Be patient and observant. Learn about each other's need for privacy. Learn to be accessible as well. In many ways, retirement is like getting married all over again. You are facing a new life and, probably, are new people. Take the time to get to know each other once again.

You might remember conversations that you had with your spouse a decade ago, or two decades ago, when you were dreaming about retirement. He/she may have described dreams and hopes that are irrelevant today. Pull out old conversations and revisit old dreams. Update your mental files on what brings a smile to your spouse's face and what bores her to tears.

INTIMACY

Take time to be intimate with your spouse. Give him or her your undivided attention. Touch each other. Sit close. Look into her eyes as you listen. Hold his hand when you sit together. Piece together memories of your significant life events. ("Remember when Rachel was born?") Look through picture albums. ("What was that place we ate when Randy spilled his drink and...") Concentrate on the good times, the times you came through for each other, the times you were totally on each other's side.

Take time to complete sentences with each other such as:

- One thing I've always appreciated about you is...
- I have always hoped when we retired we could go to...
- A lesson I've learned from you through the years is...
- One of my strongest memories of you is when...
- I knew I wanted to spend my life with you when...
- My favorite memory of you with the children was...
- My favorite vacation was...
- I was most proud of you when...
- I think our greatest accomplishment as a couple was...
- This is what I remember about our first date...
- I first realized you would be special in my life when...
- If I could re-create just one of our nights together, it would be the night we...
- The time I missed you the most was when...

Time to Date

WIDE ANGLE

"To be honest, by the time I retired Beverly and I had drifted apart. We had gotten used to our separate worlds. When we were suddenly face-to-face so much of the time, I felt as shy as I did when we first started dating. I even remember feeling nervous when I took her hand as we watched TV together. It's funny how life ebbs and flows. For us retirement means we're dating again and we like what we're finding in each other."
—Ted, Hope, Idaho

- If I could give every other man one of your traits, it would be…
- I felt closest to God, as a couple, when we…
- If there was a time in our lives that I would like to revisit, it would be…

GREEN BANANAS

One of the keys to enjoying your retirement is in planning ahead. While it is true that you are facing the last phase of your life, people are living longer and longer. There is an old joke that a person who doesn't want to plan ahead shouldn't buy green bananas. Make a commitment to your spouse that you will both enjoy each other as long as possible. Buy your bananas very green as a reminder that you have much ahead of you.

PLANNING ACTIVITIES WITH YOUR FAMILY

Use your retirement as an opportunity to spend time with your adult children and grandchildren. Build positive memories. Have conversations about things that matter. Share with them your wishes for after you are gone. Share with them your living will. Let them know what they have meant to you either through letters or conversations. Take time to be with them one-on-one rather than always in a group. Do one of these activities:

- Work a jigsaw puzzle.
- Get together around holidays—make plans for the least stressful time for everybody involved (you can celebrate a little early or late).
- Rent a condo together in the mountains or at the beach.
- Spend time with the grandkids one at a time.
- Spend time with your adult children one at a time.
- Take one of your children with you to a spiritual retreat.
- Attend your grandchildren's sports events.
- Take time to go through picture albums and begin to pass on some memory albums to your children.
- Go for walks together and remember the best moments between you.
- Call sometimes just to check in and say hi.

YOUR CHILDREN

Retirement is a time for tying up loose ends. If you have unfinished business with your children, you don't have to drag all of you through unpleasant times all over again. Nevertheless, it might be freeing to recognize that there were difficult times and to admit your wish that those times hadn't happened. Concentrate on your best moments.

Start written notes or conversations with statements such as:

- My favorite memory of you growing up is…
- I've always thought that one of your greatest strengths is…
- I thought you were so brave when I watched you…
- My most positive memory of our time together was when…
- I thought you showed such character when you…
- One of the things I've always enjoyed about you as a person is…

Once a Dad…

THE BOTTOM LINE

"One of the dangers of getting old is that you feel like you don't matter much anymore. I think this makes you sort of careless with your relationships, even the important ones. I'll never forget, which is saying a lot, when my son and I were fishing at the beach. Out of the blue I started telling him how proud I was of him. We weren't really looking at each other—we were just two guys sitting on the pier. Later though, he wrote me and told me how much what I said meant to him. I had forgotten that my opinion mattered to him. I guess a dad is always a dad."
—Dave, Naperville, Illinois

Ask questions such as:

- When did you feel the proudest of yourself growing up?
- What has been your favorite moment as an adult?
- When did you know that you were in love with your spouse and wanted to spend your life with them?
- What was it like when you found out you were going to have a child?
- What has been your most difficult decision since you've been on your own?
- What do you like best about your life?
- Who were the adults outside of our family that were most significant to you as you were growing up?
- What do you hope to do when you retire?
- What would you change about your life if you could?

As a parent you have a power for all of your life to bestow blessings on your children and grandchildren. Take time during your retirement to build moments of blessing into your conversations and interactions. Be deliberate about investing in a legacy of goodwill.

THE RV WORLD

Recreational vehicles (RVs) provide the best of both worlds. You can see the sights during the day and yet go to sleep in your own bed every night. For some people it's the best of every world.

The term RV actually applies to several kinds of vehicles:

- Motor-homes (don't need to be pulled by a car or truck, gasoline-powered, built on a chassis)
- Bus and van conversions (conversions speak for themselves, but buses are usually diesel-powered)
- Travel trailers (an RV "box" pulled by a car or truck)
- Fifth-wheel trailers (a trailer pulled by a pickup truck hooked together much like an 18-wheeler)
- Pickup campers (a camper mounted onto a pickup truck)
- Tent trailers or pop-ups (a tent that sets up in minutes on a trailer chassis and can be towed by a pickup)

WOW!

The New World

"Honestly, I never would have believed this would be us driving around in this Roadtrek. And believe it or not, at first we had a big Winnebago. We tried hotels. We tried staying at home. We've tried it all. But this just suits us best. We have the comforts of home with wheels. It's like a grownup version of the little red wagon we all had as kids. And it's really neat how when you stay at a campground it's sort of like a little community. We don't really get lonely because we can just look across our fire and see someone else living it up like we do. It's just a good thing you don't find out about these kinds of things until you retire, or we might never have owned a home."
—Barb, Santa Fe, New Mexico

If you want to see if it's the best for you, try renting an RV for a vacation. You can often rent one for the same cost as a median-priced hotel room and try out the RV lifestyle. What you will find is that there is a whole floating community out there of RVers who know the ropes and are glad to share. They'll tell you about caravaning clubs, the best campsites, emergency roadside assistance, and which discounts really give you the best rates. If you enjoy a road trip, this may be the vacation or retirement lifestyle for you.

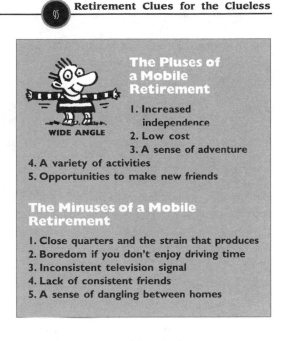

The Pluses of a Mobile Retirement

WIDE ANGLE

1. Increased independence
2. Low cost
3. A sense of adventure
4. A variety of activities
5. Opportunities to make new friends

The Minuses of a Mobile Retirement

1. Close quarters and the strain that produces
2. Boredom if you don't enjoy driving time
3. Inconsistent television signal
4. Lack of consistent friends
5. A sense of dangling between homes

RVs are actually a modern version of the wagon trains of the old west. They came into existence in the early nineteenth century as a toy for the very, very rich. The first RVing club was the Tin Can Tourists, founded in 1919. The original version of the RV was large and lavishly decked out. Today, they come in all shapes, sizes, and prices. You can find them as small as a van or as large as a mobile home. You can get them as fancy or basic as you like.

Making the Decision

The first step to deciding for a mobile retirement is to make sure it is what you and your spouse BOTH want—not just agree to, but really, really want.

Keep in mind that you can really be as mobile as you want. You can be a vacationer and just use the rig when you head out of town. You can be a part-timer or snowbird and just live in the rig part of the year. You can also be a full-timer and kiss a permanent address good-bye.

Once you agree that you want to try it, you have to face reality that what you are proposing is actually a reduction of living space by about 90 percent. You will need to be organized and you will need to be streamlined.

Where Do You Stay On The Road?

There are basically three places to park an RV:

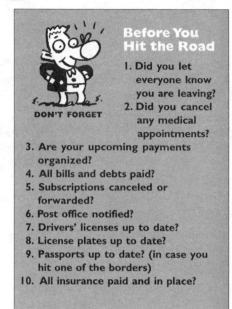

Before You Hit the Road

DON'T FORGET

1. Did you let everyone know you are leaving?
2. Did you cancel any medical appointments?
3. Are your upcoming payments organized?
4. All bills and debts paid?
5. Subscriptions canceled or forwarded?
6. Post office notified?
7. Drivers' licenses up to date?
8. License plates up to date?
9. Passports up to date? (in case you hit one of the borders)
10. All insurance paid and in place?

1. Public campgrounds (There are many directories available with detailed information.)

2. Private campgrounds, like KOA, or denominational campgrounds (usually more expensive than the public ones)

3. Freebies (truck stops, shopping plazas, rest areas, picnic sites, dead-end roads, a friend's driveway)

Of the public and private camp-grounds, some will offer full hookup (water, sewage, and electricity) and some will offer partial hookups (no electricity).

The use of RVs has grown and grown and grown and shows no sign of stopping. So what do you say? Are you up for a ride into retirement?

CATCH A CLUE

National Perks at National Parks

The federal government has a wonderful plan for how you can spend your travel dollars. Stay at a national park! And as long as you bring proof of age, there are some wonderful discounts along the way that may just make a national park the most economical way for you to travel: half price on many fees and a free lifetime entrance pass. Remember to make reservations and you can even request a national directory that will help spot lesser-known parks and help you avoid the crowds. As always, though, don't feed the bears.

SECTION 6
HOBBIES

HOBBIES

HOBBIES: KIND OF WORK, KIND OF PLAY

Hobbies are not just activities. Activities are something you do. Hobbies are something you invest yourself in. You don't just take a class then walk away. You don't just try them once and then forget about it. Hobbies hold your attention. Sometimes hobbies are those things you were always interested in but, most often, couldn't make a living at so you didn't feel like you could invest time or money in them.

Well, guess what? Once you're retired, you can.

Hobbies are what we enjoy. They are what we feel passionate about. They are what intrigue us. Hobbies can be collecting. Hobbies

WOW!

An Unexpected Hobby

"My husband has always loved cars. Now I know men in general love cars, but not like my husband. He loves full-sized cars, model cars, vintage cars, and even junkyard cars! So when he retired from a pressure-filled job with a telecommunications firm, I knew where his extra time would go...to the garage. Honestly, I never knew there were so many different things to do with cars. I have to admit, though, I've actually learned to enjoy conversations about hubcaps and hood ornaments. I often travel with him to car shows and we've even talked about refurbishing our own car to show.

"I knew that Gene would need something to wrap his life around once we retired. After managing thirty employees, you don't just walk away and watch TV all day. I'm glad he has something that he enjoys, and that I'm beginning to, that gives us a sense of excitement and momentum."
—Janie, Hope, Arkansas

can be crafting. Hobbies can be sports-like or action oriented. Mostly, though, hobbies are those things that we invest time and sometimes (too much) money into for the sake of mere interest and enjoyment. These are some of the most popular hobbies today.

Art

> Oil painting
> Pen & Ink
> Pottery
> Sculpting
> Watercolors

Bicycling

Bird-watching

Collecting

> Antique toys
> Antiques of any kind
> Beanie Babies
> Paraphernalia of a specific era or occupation (cowboys or antique tools)
> Spoons

Community theatre

Genealogy

Jigsaw puzzles

Joining a barbershop quartet

Learning new skills
A new type of gardening
Construction
Farming
Gourmet cooking
Lanuages
Musical instruments

Motorcycling

Photography

Put together models

Refinishing furniture

Other Misc.
Camping
Hiking
Remote control planes
Row-boating
Sailing
Scuba diving
Sports-related
Take flying lessons
Walking
Weight lifting
Woodworking
Write magazine articles

HOW DO I FIND A HOBBY?

Hobbies start out as activities. They start out as something you just try. So try some things. Refinish a small piece of furniture. Do a small cross-stitch. Rent a guitar and take some lessons. Take a class. Check a book out of the library. Visit a "birds of a feather" group (people with the same interest). Visit a hobby shop or craft store. Talk to people that do something well and find out if you could do it at all.

You might end up with several hobbies rather than just one. On the other hand you might try several before you ever settle on just one. You might end up with a closet full of half-finished, once-intriguing crafts. You might drive your spouse crazy with your new "obsession." And you might have the time of your life.

CATCH A CLUE

Do Something You Love:

"I stayed at home when my children were young, but once they were in school I went to work and I've worked ever since. A few years ago when I knew retirement was approaching I began to wonder what I would do with myself when I wasn't punching a clock and trying to keep the boss happy.

"As I thought about it I remembered how much I loved to cook when the children were small. We tried new dishes all the time. Even before I retired I started taking some cooking classes at our local community college. Now that I'm retired I actually teach some classes myself!"
—Esther, Kearny, Nebraska

HELPFUL HINTS

1. Don't expect your hobby to replace your life's vocation. You may still miss

work, and a hobby won't bring you the same rewards: You're not getting paid or promoted.

2. Be realistic about the expense. Talk to someone who is doing it.

3. Be realistic about the time involved.

4. Talk to your spouse. Make sure he or she understands the commitment you are about to make.

5. Make sure you have the space needed without cramping everyone.

SECTION 7
FEELIN' FINE!

THE GREAT COVER-UP

Do you recall seeing the Revlon commercial where actress Melanie Griffith says, "Don't lie about your age; defy it"? By buying that line of makeup, you can somehow "defy" the aging process by "looking" young. However, once you take the makeup off, then what?

The old adage "You're as young as you feel" really has to do with being healthy. Good physical health is one of the components of a successful retired life. Another component is accepting where you are at this time of your life. This is the way to "defy" the so-called "rigors" of getting older.

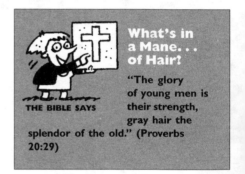

What's in a Mane. . . of Hair?

THE BIBLE SAYS

"The glory of young men is their strength, gray hair the splendor of the old." (Proverbs 20:29)

Keeping healthy includes exercising regularly, getting regular medical checkups, eating properly, and identifying and dealing with stress points in your life. Here are some suggestions for each.

EXERCISE

Remember, "your body is a temple of the Holy Spirit" (1 Corinthians 6:19). It is one of God's best creations. That means you owe it to yourself (and God!) to keep it running well! Many people balk at the thought of exercising or keeping healthy in general. This is mainly because they don't see health maintenance as a "fun" task. "It means cutting out what I like," some may say. That's not necessarily true. For exercise, you can. . .

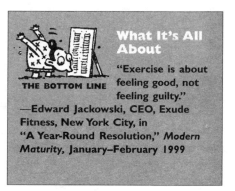

THE BOTTOM LINE

What It's All About

"Exercise is about feeling good, not feeling guilty."
—Edward Jackowski, CEO, Exude Fitness, New York City, in "A Year-Round Resolution," *Modern Maturity*, January–February 1999

Do What You Like

Who says that exercise has to be a chore? The more you enjoy an activity, the more you'll do it. If you like to swim, think about taking a daily swim or swim three times a week at your local health club or YMCA. One woman took an early swim at a Y near her home every morning at six. Not only was swimming a good choice of exercise for her, it also helped her make new friends.

Like to walk? Then take a brisk walk out in nature or in a mall. Many people of all ages walk around local malls. Many malls open their doors early just for that purpose. If there is no mall close by, walk around your neighborhood or head for the nearest forest preserve or nature trail. If you don't like the outdoors, a treadmill may be just the piece of equipment you need.

Like to ride bicycles? Dust off that bike in the garage and go for a ride or pull the clothes off the stationary bike and burn those calories! You might also think about taking up a sport or hobby. For example, learn to inline skate, play tennis or golf, or take up ballroom dancing.

Join a Health Club or YMCA
A health club or Y offers many types of exercise options. Best of all, trained personnel are on hand to help you choose a program and work the equipment. Take time to investigate the health club that best fits your lifestyle. For example, if you don't like the frenetic pace of those Bally Total Fitness commercials, opt for a low-impact program or a health club with a more laid-back approach. Many community park districts also offer

Be Still My Heart

"My flesh and my heart may fail, but God is THE BIBLE SAYS the strength of my heart and my portion forever." (Psalm 73:26)

exercise classes where you might feel more comfortable. Ask around and see if you can observe a litle bit before investing your money somewhere.

Start Off Slowly
If you really want to start maintaining a healthy body through regular exercise, don't run before you can walk. In other words, hold off on entering that bike marathon until you know you can ride a mile without having to stop every few feet to rest! If you bite off more exercise than you can chew, you'll tire more easily, risk injury, and become discouraged. Exercising twenty to thirty minutes a day, three times a week is a manageable goal you can shoot for.

See Your Doctor

Your doctor knows the type of health maintenance program that best fits your lifestyle. Before leaping into a program, consult your doctor. She can tell you whether the changes you are considering will truly benefit you or not.

Is There a Doctor in the House?

Don't like your doctor? Call a service like I-800-DOCTORS or I-800-DENTIST to investigate other doctors. Or ask a friend for a referral.

CATCH A CLUE

Exercise or sport you'll try:

_____

When _____

REGULAR CHECKUPS

If you own a car, you take it in regularly to have the oil changed and whatever else the car needs to ensure its maintenance. Seeing your doctor, dentist, and ophthalmologist (if you wear glasses) on a regular basis is a required part of any health maintenance program. If heart disease, diabetes, cataracts, cancer (prostate, ovarian, or other), hypertension, and other medical conditions run in your family, you owe it to yourself to have yourself checked from stem to stern.

REGULAR CHECKUPS ALSO INCLUDE:

Doing Self-Checks

The National Stroke Association recommends a heartbeat self-check once a month for those at risk of strokes. To do a self-check, put two fingers against the wrist; press until you can feel a pulse. As you monitor your pulse for about

Knee-jerk Reaction?

"When your knees buckle and your belt won't." —George Burns, "Some Signs That Old Age Might Be Creeping Up on You," in *Coming of Age Gracefully*

WOW!

30 seconds, tap your foot to the rhythm. Doing this once a month can alert you to irregularities in beats. If you discern an irregularity, inform your doctor.

If you're a female, you should also do a breast self-check. Usually when a woman reaches the age of thirty-five, she should begin having a mammogram regularly. Talk to your doctor about your risk level. If you're high risk, you could check for lumps once a week. Otherwise, a woman should check for lumps every month. If you notice anything unusual, see your doctor immediately.

Check your blood pressure also. You can purchase a blood pressure kit from many drugstores or department stores. Many drugstores also offer monthly checks right in the store.

Reevaluating Your Medication

Your body goes through changes from year to year. If you've been taking medication for several years, you might need to evaluate whether the potency of your medication is continuing to give you what you need. One woman found that she did not need to take as much medication for hypertension as she did in the past. If you can cut down on medication, that's a plus!

Following through on Your Doctor's Advice

This may seem like common sense, but it bears repeating. If your doctor tells you to follow certain procedures to lose weight, lower your cholesterol, exercise, or whatever, he or she expects you to follow through. No one can do this for you. Rather than self-

The Blue and the Gray. . . Hair?

"In the years before the Civil War, therefore, Americans respected the nation's older men and women because of their age, their wisdom, and their experience." —W. Andrew Achenbaum, *Images of Old Age in America 1790 to the Present*

diagnose your problems or tell yourself, "My doctor doesn't know what he or she is talking about," follow through on the medical advice you're given. If, for some reason, you doubt the wisdom of your doctor's advice, get a second opinion or choose another doctor.

Your next doctor's appointment is _____

EATING PROPERLY

During the 80s everyone went bran crazy. Suddenly bran was everywhere and in everything. "Fiber is good!" and "Eat more fiber" we were told. The "fat free" craze kicked into high gear during the 80s and 90s. Americans are still health conscious, and with good reason. After all, "You are what you eat." Many of us, if we were honest, would say we're a Big Mac and fries or a gooey pizza with every-thing (with a bran muffin for dessert, of course)!

You know what you need to maintain a proper diet. Eat foods that are lower in cholesterol and sugar. Eat fruits and vegetables. Cut down on fats. Don't skip meals. Does this mean you have to eat what you don't like for the rest of your life? Nope. It just means being sensible about what you do eat.

AARP

CATCH A CLUE

If you need more information on retirement, call The American Association of Retired Persons (AARP) at 1-800-424-5410. Check out *Modern Maturity*, the monthly magazine of AARP.

IDENTIFYING AND DEALING WITH STRESS

What is stress? It is basically your reaction to the challenges of your life. Hans Selye, the first doctor to study stress, calls it "the rate of wear and tear on the body." Stress has a direct effect on your physical health. Stress can give you a temporary amount of energy to undertake a task, but after-ward, you feel drained. Failure to deal with chronic stress in healthy ways can lead to long-term health problems.

What are the stressors of your life? Take time to evaluate what causes you stress. A certain amount of stress is normal, but once you climb over that amount, life becomes difficult. Of the stressors mentioned below, how many have you undergone within the past year? six months? week? Use the points in the right column to determine the amount of stress you have undergone (50–60 is about a normal stress load).

Sources of stress	Points
Death of a spouse	100
Divorce	75
Change in job situation (downsizing, retirement)	50
Family crises (adult child moves home; husband's insomnia)	30 each
Health problems (your own)	30 each
Major life events (weddings, births, graduations, remarriage)	10 each

Your score _____

Now check the list of stress-coping mechanisms below. If you have turned to any of these sources, subtract or add the points in the right column from your score above for each time that you used that source. The lower your score, the healthier your stress management plan.

Coping with stress	Points
Support from family (church family or immediate)	-15
Relaxing hobby or deep breathing exercises	-10

Exercise	-5
Proper nutrition	-5
Proper sleep	-5
Cigarettes	+15
Alcohol	+10
Drugs	+15

Your score _____

How do you usually deal with stress? Many people unfortunately turn to unhealthy sources of stress management—alcohol, drugs, smoking—which can cause long-term health problems. The Bible provides one healthy way to deal with stress: "Do not be anxious about anything, but in everything, by prayer and petition, with thanksgiving, present your requests to God" (Philippians 4:6).

SECTION 8
INSURANCE

INSURANCE

Enjoying your retirement means planning for the eventualities you can control and preparing to face the ones you can't. Insurance can help you do that.

Insurance is not something you buy one time and leave alone. Your insurance needs change as you wade in and out of the different stages of your life. The insurance industry also changes as death rates fall and life expectancies rise. If you're anywhere over fifty years of age, you are probably considered a better health risk now than you would have been a decade ago. That can mean lower rates. It can also mean you need a more aggressive health or life insurance plan to see you through that extra decade that modern science is dangling before your bifocaled eyes.

Unfortunately, buying and managing your insurance policies can be daunting. There are the companies. Then there are the agents. Then there are the multiple policies and the options for coverage. It can be over-whelming. Here are the basic components, in terms of insurance, that you will probably want to evaluate before you retire.

HOMEOWNER'S INSURANCE

You'll need to reevaluate your homeowner's and property coverage as you approach retirement. Do you remember where your policies are? If they are difficult to understand (which ones aren't?) then call your agent and have them walk you through the policy point by point. Here are some things to remember:

- If you own a condominium ask around and become aware of the master policy that covers the complex. Don't pay to duplicate that same coverage.
- Most insurance companies are not allowed to change or terminate your insurance based only on age. They may cite risks that are related to your age bracket, though.
- You may need separate policies for vacation homes or rental property or boats or RVs. You may also need "named-peril" policies (for instance, just to cover flood) rather than broad sweeping homeowner type policies.
- Take time to look over insurance paperwork. Don't simply assume that you won't understand it and stick it in a file. Don't simply assume that if it was suitable when you bought it twenty years ago, it's still fine. Call and ask questions about the parts that seems impossibly unclear, particularly if they are related to changes in the policies or the premiums.
- If you have relatives living with you or in any of your second-home or rental properties, call your agent and ask how they might affect your liability should an accident happen in that dwelling and you need to place a claim.

AUTO INSURANCE

As with any other insurance, first of all understand your policy. Have someone at your agency sit down with you and talk you through each category of coverage. Here are some other points to keep in mind:

- You can sometimes lower your premiums by raising your deductibles or by dropping collision overage (if your car is old with a low replacement value), but DON'T drop your coverage on uninsured motorists.
- Do a little research to know whether your insurance covers rental cars. If

it does, decline the offer of insurance from the rental car agency.

- Don't give your car keys to a family member who is not covered on your insurance. Yes, it is a reasonable response even if it makes them irritated.
- Find out what kind of discount you can receive (often as much as 10 percent) by taking safe driving courses, and take them.
- Some automobile policies automatically cancel at a certain age. Be aware of that before you sign or pay.

LIFE INSURANCE

Most sources claim that about seven out of ten adults in the United States have some form of life insurance. Most of these policies involve a monthly premium that insures a benefit in case of premature death.

Your needs in regards to life insurance change as you age and as your life changes. A young father might have insurance so that if he should die at a young age his family would be cared for financially and his wife would not have to work for a number of years. As that father ages, though, he will have different needs. When he is about to retire, he may care less about premature death as he does about using the money he has invested in the policy to enjoy his life. Because of these kinds of changes, you should review your policy every few years and adjust your funds accordingly.

Here are some points to remember about life insurance:

- "Term" life insurance is for a specific period of time. When it expires there is no residual cash value.
- "Whole" life insurance involves level premiums and guaranteed cash values.
- Most kinds of life insurance policies are a combination of "term" and "whole life."
- Explore rider options that are available now such as long-term care

coverage, disability waivers, and cost of living adjustments.

- You have a grace period after you buy a policy in which you can change your mind if you realize you didn't fully understand the risks or the investment. The period may be anywhere from ten to thirty days.

- You may be able to convert your group life policy from work into an individual policy when you retire.

- Many of the rules for life insurance change as you pass age fifty. If you've had the same policy since before then, ask your agent if any adjustments need to be made.

Senior Discount

CATCH A CLUE

Always ask about senior discounts. There is often a discount of around 10–20 percent for retirees for any type of insurance (sometimes even if you still work part-time.)

Often 10 percent is taken off of auto insurance premiums for attending driving safety courses.

MISCELLANEOUS COVERAGE

Just because you don't own a home doesn't mean you don't need any insurance coverage. Loss and liability are a concern no matter what your living situation. Keep in mind that these kinds of policies are available:

Renter's Insurance
This is for the contents and sometimes also for the improvements you've made on the property.

Mobile Home Insurance
This is usually handled by niche companies, rather than the big firms. Because of that, rates may vary greatly, so check around.

Travel Insurance
Usually the cost is around $5 per $100 of coverage. As you age, this kind of insurance becomes more valuable.

Pre-need Funeral Insurance
Funerals cost thousands of dollars. You can usually pay that ahead of time through funeral insurance. You can make monthly payments or pay in a lump sum and therefore be sure that at least this burden will be taken from your family's shoulders.

SECTION 9
SHARP AS A TACK

A LABOR OF LOBE?

It is said that most humans only use about 10 percent of their brains. Gainful employment and taking care of a family are two routes many have taken to keep their minds occupied. But what happens when a person retires or all of the children leave the nest? Does that mean saying adíos to a few thousand brain cells? Hardly! Keeping in good mental health is another way to have a successful retirement. This means keeping your mind sharp. How do you do that?

WALK THE PHILIPPIANS 4:8 "THOUGHT ROAD"

Philippians 4:8 provides a road map for focusing your thoughts: "Whatever is true, whatever is noble, whatever is right, whatever is pure, whatever is lovely, whatever is admirable—if anything is excellent or praiseworthy—think about such things." In other words, think good thoughts! One

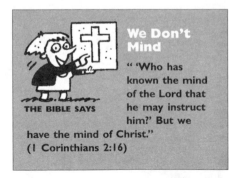

We Don't Mind

THE BIBLE SAYS

" 'Who has known the mind of the Lord that he may instruct him?' But we have the mind of Christ."
(1 Corinthians 2:16)

way to start is to keep focused on Jesus and the Word of God. Another way is to cease speculating about what could have been or what could be. Focus on what's true, noble, right, pure, lovely, and admirable.

LEARN A NEW SKILL

Who says that school is just for kids? Take a continuing education class at a community college. Take courses to brush up on your computer skills or to get into the computer revolution for the first time. Take up painting or sculpture. Auto repair. A musical instrument. A desire to learn can help you remain sharp. Anna Mary Robertson Moses, better known as Grandma Moses, *began* painting while in her *70s*. After becoming a well-known folk artist, she continued painting until her death at 101. So. . .what will *you* learn?

Never Too Late

THE BOTTOM LINE "The wonderful thing about all human life is that it is never too late to start, despite one's regret. For it is in retirement, if health allows, when freedom is a gift to each of us."—Gracia Grindal in her essay, "Reflections," in *Coming of Age Gracefully*

TAKE UP A SPORT

Sports like tennis and golf are also good for mental acuity, aside from the added health benefits. You can learn a sport at your local Y, tennis club, or golf course. Don't worry if you're not Tiger Woods by your third class!

DO ACTIVITIES TO INCREASE YOUR MENTAL ACUMEN

Crossword puzzles, trivia quizzes, and other types of puzzles are good for the brain. Daily newspapers and many magazines have puzzles of some kind. You'll find plenty of crossword puzzle books at your elbow at the supermarket checkout lanes. Many Christian publishers also publish Bible-related puzzle books. Check your local Christian bookstore for recommendations.

TAKE UP A CAUSE OR PROJECT

Now that you'll have more time, you can choose a project to work on. Volunteering is a great way to keep the mind active. How about delivering meals for the Meals on Wheels program? Or, choose a ministry you have a passion for and go at it gung ho. You might also help out at the hospital or a nursing facility.

WOW!

Keeping Active

"I do crossword puzzles. I have a jigsaw puzzle that I work on. I do crafts around the house. I like making things out of wood, like picture frames. I want to do some drawing and painting."—Sam, a recently retired teacher, Glenwood, Illinois

READ, READ, READ

Be a bookworm. Read fiction. Nonfiction. History. Tragedy. Comedy. The library can be a great place to hang out. Audiobooks are also good choices, particularly for long car trips.

TAKE UP ANOTHER LANGUAGE

Learn French. Spanish. Tagalog (the language of the Philippines). Swahili. Italian. Take a class at a community college in the conversational style of the language you choose. Then, once you're confident in that language (or even if you aren't), try out your newfound conversational skills at an ethnic restaurant.

WORK A PART-TIME JOB

"Work?" you may ask. "Why on earth would I work when I'm retired????" Good question. Some individuals take on part-time employment to keep their minds occupied. Some choose an occupation they always wanted to do. For example, one harried retail executive took on part-time employment in a car dealership. He loved cars; selling them had been his dream job for years. What's your dream job? How will you make that dream a reality?

Laughter: The Best Medicine

DON'T FORGET "It's easy to find things to complain about as we grow older, but it's so much healthier to laugh instead."—Barbara Johnson, *Living Somewhere Between Estrogen and Death*
Isn't that a wonderful title?

THINGS YOU CAN AVOID

Here is a handy list of activities you *can* avoid, now that you're retired:

Saying, "I can't learn this" or "I can't do this." Although there are certain goals a person of retirement age cannot attain (for example, becoming the youngest person ever to win an Oscar, thereby eclipsing Tatum O'Neal and Anna Paquin), there are many that *can* be reached. Remember, "I can do everything through him [Christ] who gives me strength" (Philippians 3:13).

> **Ready, Willing, and Able**
>
> "So here I am today, eighty-five years old! I am still as strong today as the day Moses sent me out; I'm just as vigorous to go out to battle now as I was then. Now give me this hill country that the LORD promised me that day. You yourself heard then that the Anakites were there. . .but, the LORD helping me, I will drive them out just as he said."—Caleb in Joshua 14:10–12

Occupying the mind with bitter thoughts or regretful memories. The apostle Paul said, "Forgetting what is behind and straining toward what is ahead, I press on toward the goal to win the prize for which God has called me heavenward in Christ Jesus" (Philippians 3:13–14). Bitterness, angry thoughts toward others, regret, and thoughts of revenge blunt the mind's energy, rather than sharpen it. Take Paul's advice. Use this new time of your life to think "whatever is lovely" as the Philippians 4:8 "Thought Road" suggests.

Allowing yourself to be manipulated into solving the unsolvable problems of others. These may include ongoing family battles by individuals who choose to allow others to fight the battles they could fight themselves. Now that you have time on your hands, you might be seen as a likely candidate to take on responsibilities others blithely shrug off. Use wisdom. Although you'll want to offer your help when someone genuinely needs it, be careful about volunteering to handle an issue only God can solve.

SECTION 10
CLOSER THAN EVER

TWO PEAS IN A POD

When many people think about retirement, they consider how they can get closer to their spouses. Want to have a successful retired life? Then also give some consideration to how you can get closer than ever with the Lord.

As a member of the workforce or as the caretaker of a family, your life was busy with your responsibilities and concerns. Now that retirement is upon you or the children have left the nest, you'll have more time to devote to your first love. As Asaph writes in Psalm 73:28: "But as for me, it is good to be near God. I have made the Sovereign LORD my refuge; I will tell of all your deeds."

How can you get closer than ever to the Lord?

REJOICE IN THE LORD

Paul starts off Philippians 3 with this admonition: "Rejoice in the Lord!" Later in the letter he remarks, "Rejoice in the Lord always. I will say it again: Re-joice!" (4:4). Obviously it was important enough to repeat. The first step to getting closer to the Lord (besides the obvious one of

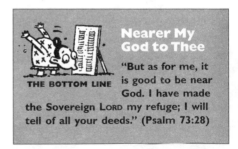

Nearer My God to Thee

THE BOTTOM LINE

"But as for me, it is good to be near God. I have made the Sovereign LORD my refuge; I will tell of all your deeds." (Psalm 73:28)

acknowledging your *need* to know Him in the first place) is to be glad that you know Him. Most parents are glad when their children want to get to know them. Your Heavenly Father is no exception.

HAVE A DAILY TIME WITH HIM

Start and end each day by His side. You might choose to go through a daily devotional that encourages your walk with Christ. Or, like many others, you might choose to read through the Bible using a one-year method. Many Bibles have a suggested reading plan for doing so. Whatever you decide to do, don't forget prayer. It's your lifeline to the Lord.

Keep in Touch

"God. . .expects us to keep in touch with Him. Know what's going on. Keep growing regardless of how old you are." —E. Jane Mall, *And God Created Wrinkles*

WOW!

JOIN A WEEKLY BIBLE STUDY

In addition to your daily time with the Lord, a weekly Bible study affords you the opportunity of learning about the Lord and meeting with other believers. You might check out those your church offers, or go to one sponsored by a different church. If you're a new believer, this is a necessary first step toward growing in your faith in the Lord. If you've been a believer for some time, you already know that this is a step you need to keep taking to continue growing in your faith in the Lord.

AUDIT A COURSE AT A CHRISTIAN COLLEGE

If there is a college nearby, think about taking a course on the New Testament or another subject that interests you. Don't be intimidated by how much you think you might need to know in order to take the class. (That's why auditing is a good option.)

Finding Time

"I'm involved in a lot of church-related activities. I'm on the finance committee, I'm a deacon and a trustee. We have a lot of meetings. My church involvement has increased (since I've been retired). I go to the fellowship hall to watch football and do Bible studies on Monday nights. I'm still trying to hang loose and sort things out and figure out where I want to devote more of my time."
—Sam, Glenwood, Illinois

KEEP MATTERS RIGHT BETWEEN YOU AND GOD

Good spiritual health also includes making sure matters are A-OK between you and God. This means being quick to confess wrongdoing and even quicker to ask for forgiveness. The old saying, "Confession is good for the soul" is certainly true. As David said, "Blessed is the man whose sin the LORD does not count against him and in whose spirit is no deceit. When I kept silent, my bones wasted away through my groaning all day long" (Psalm 32:2–3).

CULTIVATE A THANKFUL ATTITUDE

A thankful, uncomplaining spirit is always near and dear to God's heart. It's also a sure sign that God is in control of your life. As David wrote in several of the psalms, "Give thanks to the LORD, call on his name." Being thankful reminds us to concentrate on who God is and what He's done, rather than on what He *hasn't* done or about what we think He's done "incorrectly."

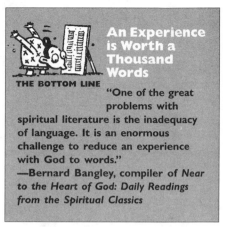

THE BOTTOM LINE

An Experience is Worth a Thousand Words

"One of the great problems with spiritual literature is the inadequacy of language. It is an enormous challenge to reduce an experience with God to words."
—Bernard Bangley, compiler of *Near to the Heart of God: Daily Readings from the Spiritual Classics*

READ CHRISTIAN LIVING BOOKS

If you're a reader, take in a work by an author who is close to the Lord and wants to encourage you to draw close to Him too. Your local Christian bookstore has dozens waiting for your perusal. Don't be afraid to ask for recommendations. You can also check out catalogs from Christian publishers to glean their latest offerings. Remember, though: A book is not meant to be a substitute for reading the Word.

HANG OUT WITH OTHER CHRISTIANS

How can hanging out with other people help you draw closer to the Lord? Well, other Christians can encourage you in your walk. Hearing about others' triumphs and tribulations in their walks can help you grow.

GET INTO THE HABIT

It is said that a habit takes at least twenty-one days to develop. For the next twenty-one days, what steps will you take to build the habit of sticking close to the Lord? You might use a notebook or prayer journal to keep track of your progress.

WOW!

The Best Part

"Better than the handiwork of God, dear heart, is God himself."

—Walter Wangerin, Jr. in his essay "When You Get There, Wait," in *Coming of Age Gracefully*

SECTION 11
PLAYING CATCH-UP

SILVER AND GOLD

No discussion of retirement can be complete without touching on the importance of maintaining one's social health. Remember that old adage:

Sticky Friends

"There is a friend who sticks closer than a brother."
(Proverbs 18:24)

THE BIBLE SAYS

> *Make new friends, but keep the old.*
> *One is silver and the other's gold.*

Old friends are priceless commodities. New ones are too. If you want to have a successful retired life, you can't neglect this area. As the Bible says, "Do not forsake your friend and the friend of your father" (Proverbs 27:10). Here are some people who realized this.

MEET PRESTON AND SUSIE WASHINGTON

When Preston turned fifty-five, he and his wife Susie sold their house in Chicago to move to Missouri City, Texas. While in Chicago, they had been part of a large group of close friends from church who met regularly for brunch or to go out to dinner. Having become part of a large church in Sugarland, Texas, the Washingtons met several new people, particularly within their large Sunday school class. (Everything is big in Texas!) They began socializing with them and soon developed the habit of going out for brunch with them after church every Sunday. The Washingtons and some of their new friends also began to minister regularly at a local retirement home.

But what about their old friends back in Chicago? Did they just ditch them? No! In fact, they are closer than ever to their old friends. Why? One word—commitment. They keep a list nearby to remind them of upcoming birthdays and anniversaries. They also visit their friends whenever they can. One summer, a group of friends from Chicago rented a van and drove down to Texas for a visit. Now that's commitment!

Friends for Life

"A friend loves at all times." (Proverbs 17:17)

WIDE ANGLE

MEET TRUDI GEHRING

Trudi Gehring, who lives in Indiana, retired from her job as a house mother at Concordia University. Never one to let grass grow under her feet, Trudi acquired a computer when she was eighty-five. After her nephew taught her the basics, Trudi was able to keep in touch with her son in Hong Kong and grandchildren via E-mail. She sends letters by snail mail to old friends who don't have computers. As an added bonus, Trudi and her husband Ron play cards regularly with friends.

YOUR TURN

Making and keeping friends takes a concentrated effort on both parts. Here are ways you can keep up with old friends near and far and make new ones:

ASK GOD FOR THE COURAGE TO CONNECT

Many times, people don't make new friends or keep up with old ones because they're afraid of connecting with others. Ask the Lord to help you reach out to others. Then ask Him for the determination and endurance to maintain these relationships. It *will* take work!

PHONE FIRST

The advertising slogan "Long distance is the next best thing to being there" is true. If you live far away, make a habit of calling old friends (and new ones) and keeping them up to date with your life. Then make an effort to visit in person every once in awhile.

WRITE LETTERS

A letter is always a wonderful, treasured item. You don't have to wait until Christmas to think about sending a letter. Send letters anytime via snail mail or E-mail. Don't forget to send recent pictures of yourself or the

WOW!

Filling the Void

"I retired early from my job as a public school-teacher (middle grades fourth through sixth). I belong to a bridge club with some of my old coworkers. We play once a month on Friday nights. I also bowl on two leagues (winter leagues). We (some of the other teachers) just started a retirement club where we get together once a month on a Wednesday evening. We've met twice so far. We anticipate traveling together and going shopping; you know, just doing little things to keep from being so bored, because you *do* miss the job some. When you get together with people, it fills in the space."

—**Lillie, Glenwood, Illinois**

grandchildren along. If you have a scanner, you can scan photos in and attach them to be downloaded later.

GO TO REUNIONS

High school, college, and family reunions are great ways to reconnect, to talk about who's looking "old" (not *you,* of course), and have fun at the same time. If you can, bring photos from the past to share. Don't forget the video camera!

DO VOLUNTEER OR PART-TIME WORK

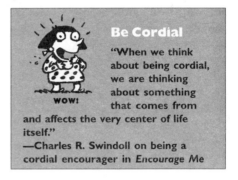

Be Cordial

"When we think about being cordial, we are thinking about something that comes from and affects the very center of life itself."
—**Charles R. Swindoll on being a cordial encourager in** *Encourage Me*

Volunteer and part-time work, as was mentioned in the section "Sharp as a Tack," can open up a whole new area of friendships. Help out at the hospital. Shelve books at the library. Bag groceries at the supermarket. Be willing to serve and be accessible.

EXTEND HOSPITALITY TOWARD OTHERS

Open up your home to new friends and old. Invite people over for a meal or just for coffee. Turn your home into a center for the encouragement and building up of others. (See Ephesians 4:29.)

EXTEND FRIENDSHIP PARAMETERS

A friend can be someone within your age group or without. Get involved with young children. Get to know college students. Fellowship with younger married couples. Sit under the wisdom of someone older than you. Don't assume that someone younger or older won't want your friendship and the qualities you have to offer. You've got a lot to offer! Why not start. . .today?

WOW!

The Adjustment

"Up to now, I've kind of backed away (from old coworkers). Right now I'm in the calling stage, rather than participating in activities. I'm coming down off a high almost. It's such a dramatic and sudden change, you know, from an almost regimented life. It's taken some adjusting. But I'm getting used to it."
—Sam, Glenwood, Illinois

SECTION 12

VOLUNTEERING AND PART-TIME JOBS

WHY VOLUNTEER?

How many times during your working life do you wish that you had time to "really help," to not care so much about the "bottom line." But, the truth is, when you are working to pay your bills, the bottom line matters. That is why volunteering is such a wonderful option for retirees. With a lifetime of experience and expertise behind them and years of time and energy ahead of them, they are people with a lot to offer and, hopefully, the time and inclination to do it.

For some retirees volunteering works best in the same arena in which they were employed. In this way a worker christens his work anew by offering it to his church or community free of charge. A building contractor can volunteer for Habitat for Humanity. A social worker can provide advice and support for the homeless. A nurse can volunteer at the hospital.

But for others, volunteering is a time to try that new thing, to use that unused gift, to explore abilities that you didn't have time to explore while you were working to pay the electric bill. Sometimes the nurse needs to try her hand at building a house for an underprivileged family. Sometimes the building contractor excels at volunteering in the pediatrics ward. Sometimes the social worker relishes pulling out the clarinet and playing her heart out in the volunteer orchestra at church. Volunteering is a way to give back to the community, but it is just as often a way to develop yourself and enjoy learning new skills.

You are also taking care of yourself when you volunteer. It's the "staying active" quotient. Being a part of a team, learning new skills, feeling good about your contribution, even just having to get up in the morning and get going—all these things keep you younger and sharper. Volunteering is a reminder that we are all needed.

TRADE IN YOUR JOB

One of the challenges of retirement is giving up that activity called "our job" that defined us and determined our level of success, our valid place in our community and in society as a whole. After retirement volunteering can do the same thing. The financial reward is not there to judge success by, but there are other rewards just waiting to be found.

Find out about the existing volunteer needs in your community; at the

WIDE ANGLE

Finding Something to Enjoy

Volunteering should be a joy to you. If it's not, then it's just unpaid work. To give you the greatest potential for enjoyment, think first about what you like to do, then match that passion with the needs that are out there.

- If you like to sing or play an instrument, play for the residents of a nursing home or hospital.
- If you like to cook, volunteer at a soup kitchen.
- If you like to play sports, coach Little League or for the boy's club.
- If you like to be outdoors, work with the Boy Scouts or parks and recreation.
- If you like to read, then work with literacy or volunteer to read aloud at the children's library.
- If you like to write, volunteer to work on the newsletter or the brochure of a nonprofit organization.
- If you like to teach, teach crafts at a nursing home or teach English as a second language.

same time, think of what you'd like to do for an organization and make a proposal. It seldom hurts to ask. If they don't need the service you offer, offer it somewhere else.

IDEAS FOR COMMUNITY INVOLVEMENT

Schools: tutoring or after-school education (from Head Start to adult continuing education)

The American Red Cross

Talent Bank of the AARP

The Salvation Army

Local museums or libraries

Habitat for Humanity

The YMCA and YWCA

Meals on Wheels or other similar programs

Boy Scouts or Girl Scouts

Camp Fire Boys and Girls

Retired and Senior Volunteer Program (RSVP)

National Park Services (info desks, guiding tours, maintaining trails)

National Executive Service Corps (NESC)

Lion's Clubs

Shriner's Clubs

Volunteering

"I never knew I would enjoy volunteering so much. I worked hard all my life as an elementary schoolteacher. I promised myself when I retired that I would travel and see the world and do all the things I hadn't had time to do. But then, one opportunity came up and then another. First an opportunity to volunteer in the pediatrics ward of the hospital. Then an opportunity to lead some spiritual retreats for my church. I never knew I could have so much fun and at the same time feel like I'm really making a difference in my community."
—Mary Tucker, age 68, Paterson, New Jersey

Literacy volunteers

Sports leagues and teams

Special Olympics

Parent-Teacher Organizations

Junior Achievement

Ad Litem programs for children who need to be accompanied into court

Ushers or crews for community theatres

Library assistants

Receptionists for nonprofit organizations and clinics

Crossing guards for school systems

Information centers for city organizations or visitors' bureaus

Hospitals

Centers for the handicapped

Battered women's shelters

Goodwill Industries

Soup kitchens and homeless shelters

Foster grandparents' programs at many schools and churches

Adopt-a-college-student programs at many churches

Big Brother/Big Sister Programs

Part-Timer

WIDE ANGLE

"My wife and I would have driven each other crazy if we had both retired and faced each other every day of the week! As it turned out, I have continued to work for my company but on a contract, part-time basis. It was easier for them than training somebody new. My wife volunteers twenty hours a week at our church and she just loves it. We stay busy enough that we welcome our time at home together and we always have lots to talk about and catch up on. For us, this is a great way to be retired."
—Bob Samms, age 66, Atlanta, Georgia

Children's hospitals

Hospitality houses such as the Ronald McDonald House

Children's and youth shelters

Neighborhood watches

Assistance to the visually impaired

Companions for the handicapped

Disease-related associations: Leukemia Foundation, Muscular Dystrophy
Association, National Easter Seal Society, National Multiple Sclerosis
Society, Spinal Cord Injury Association, Cerebral Palsy Association,
American Cancer Society, Alzheimer's Association, Arthritis Founda-
tion, American Heart Association, American Diabetes Association, etc.

Animal shelters, humane societies

Veterans' hospitals and organizations

Audubon Society

Local hospice organizations

Local blood banks

Voting polls

WHY FIND A PART-TIME JOB?

You grow up in the workplace. You find your stride. You work hard. You get
promoted. You figure out what makes your boss tick, what makes the
numbers crunch. You build a reputation. You receive merit raises. You are
recognized for distinguished service.

Then you retire. And you don't work anymore?

For some people that works, but for others, there is just no way to stop
cold turkey. In our culture our work defines part, if not all, of who we are. It

gives us a reason to get up in the morning. It gives us the benefit of insurance and of acquaintances. And sometimes, whether we admit it or not, it's fun. So while retirement is a wonderful stage of life, it doesn't mean you can't work. It just means you probably don't have to work as hard.

For the retired person a part-time job is a wonderful halfway point between being the employee and being the unemployed.

That's the good news. The best news is that in today's world the retired adult is a sought-after commodity in many markets. Businesses are aware that retired adults offer some of the same benefits as students: They enjoy flexible schedules and are not so concerned with the corporate ladder. But unlike students, retired adults are more settled, responsible people with (hopefully) well-developed problem-solving skills. As long as the work is not physically intensive, who could be a better fit?

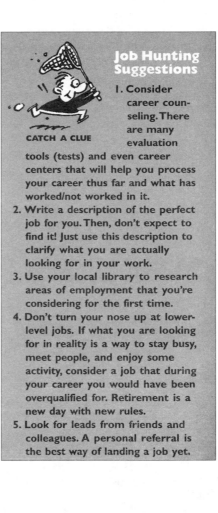

CATCH A CLUE

Job Hunting Suggestions

1. Consider career counseling. There are many evaluation tools (tests) and even career centers that will help you process your career thus far and what has worked/not worked in it.
2. Write a description of the perfect job for you. Then, don't expect to find it! Just use this description to clarify what you are actually looking for in your work.
3. Use your local library to research areas of employment that you're considering for the first time.
4. Don't turn your nose up at lower-level jobs. If what you are looking for in reality is a way to stay busy, meet people, and enjoy some activity, consider a job that during your career you would have been overqualified for. Retirement is a new day with new rules.
5. Look for leads from friends and colleagues. A personal referral is the best way of landing a job yet.

But be warned. Whether you are retired or employed, you will find it's easier to find a job (even part-time) if you have a job. If you think you might like to work part-time after retirement, start looking before you retire. You may even ask your current employer about part-time opportunities there.

IF IT HAD BEEN A SNAKE. . .

Perhaps the first place you should look for part-time work is at your current place of employment. There are many part-time arrangements that you can offer. These kinds of arrangements give the employer a more experienced candidate and give you added freedom.

If you pursue this kind of part-time situation, remember to ask clearly how your benefits will be affected by your decrease in hours, and be sure you understand how your pay will affect your pension.

OTHER PLACES TO LOOK

Many retirees start their own business rather than working part-time (or full-time) for someone else. Who hasn't heard about Colonel Sanders who didn't even start KFC until he was sixty-five years old? Retirement may be the perfect time for you to pursue your dream, to turn a hobby into a thriving business.

Before you decide to pursue this avenue, though, think long and hard. Here are some questions you should definitely know the answer to before starting your own business:

1. Do you have the money to invest in this business?

2. Does this fit in with your spouse's goals for retirement?

3. Do you REALLY want the pressure of being the place where the buck ALWAYS stops?

4. Do you have a good handle on how much of your time this will take?

These are organizations that specialize in helping seniors find work if they want it:

- State Employment Agency
- Local Area Agency on Aging
- The National Council on the Aging
- Operation ABLE
- AARP
- The Senior Community Service Employment Program
- Forty Plus Clubs
- Older Women's League

These are the kinds of places that often hire retirees on a part-time basis:

- Retails stores (greeters)
- Fast-food restaurants

DON'T FORGET

Before the Interview

1. Learn to value your own expertise. Above all, don't apologize for your age.
2. Don't use a resume if it's not necessary.
3. Set the tone for the interview in the first five minutes. Eye contact and a firm handshake go a long way.
4. Leave the picture of the grand-children at home.
5. Don't spend too much time talking about your "glory days" if they were more than ten years ago.
6. Use actual numbers/statistics as much as possible. ("While I was in that sales position, sales increased 50 percent.")
7. Be comfortable in your own skin. If you aren't, if you try to be someone that you are not, it won't work.

- Family style restaurants
- Museums
- Consignment shops
- Antique stores
- Small retail businesses
- Interim management agencies
- Grocery stores

You might also consider tempo-rary employment agencies who need to place experienced workers in temporary slots. You always have the option of refusing a job, but if you prove yourself you'll always be asked again.

Bright Lights

These cities have been known for being the best locations for finding part-time work:

Orlando, Florida
Phoenix, Arizona
West Palm Beach, Florida
Hollywood, Florida
San Diego, California
Austin, Texas
Las Vegas, Nevada
Miami, Florida
Fort Myers, Florida
San Antonio, Texas
Portsmouth, New Hampshire
Myrtle Beach, South Carolina
Carson City, Nevada
Salinas, California

SECTION 13
LEGAL PAPERWORK

PREPARING A WILL

TALKING ABOUT THE UNMENTIONABLES

You're right if you believe that thinking about and talking about your will involves some unpleasant eventualities. Inherent in the conversation, whether it is with yourself or your spouse or your children, is your own death. Who relishes dealing with their own mortality?

But the reality is that just as you manage your "stuff" (your possessions, your money, your property) now, SOMEONE is going to have to do SOMETHING with that stuff after you are gone. On one hand, preparing your will is a last act of responsibility, your last vestige of control over the physical accumulation of your life. On the other hand, every decision you

THE BOTTOM LINE

A Glossary

You're going to be dealing with legal documents and, probably, attorneys. So here's a basic vocab lesson to help you through.

ESTATE: ALL your "stuff," your assets and possessions (including money and property)

EXECUTOR: the person responsible for carrying out the wishes in your will. He or she does not have to be an attorney. Usually the executor is a spouse, family member, or close friend. If your estate is a complicated one, for instance, if you have a family-owned business, you might choose an institution such as a bank for your executor.

GUARDIAN: the person responsible for a minor or minors (they are given guardianship)

PROBATE: the legal process of settling your estate, particularly the property you own when you die. A probate judge is the one who makes decisions about what your last wishes, as they are written in your will, mean for the ones you've left behind.

refuse to make now, leaves a decision someone will have to make later. Your family will have enough to deal with losing you; will they be in the best frame of mind to disburse your goods in the midst of that crisis time?

SPEAKING OF FAMILY. . .

Even in the best-case scenarios, family decision making can be a difficult thing. Enter into that heightened emotions, funeral arrangements and expenses, sums of money, objects with great sentimental worth, and any lingering intrafamily rivalry, and you've got the sum total of a difficult time. One of the best things that you can do for your family NOW is take the responsibility of letting your wishes, in regards to your stuff, be known. This is true no matter how far away from retirement you may be in terms of years. Ask your family NOW what part of your legacy is important to them to share. Deal with feelings now. Don't leave any land mines or surprises.

GETTING DOWN TO BUSINESS

You should have three main concerns in preparing your will:
1. How will your assets be distributed? Who gets what and how much?
2. Are your assets in the best condition to be distributed easily? Does your car need to be changed into your spouse's name? Do you have real estate going to someone who really will need cash? Can you go ahead and sell? Can you go ahead and put cash into a security?
3. Will your family get the most out of your estate? How much will be subject to governmental taxes? Every state is different and your will must be created in accordance with the laws of your state. A good rule of thumb is that in most states an estate of $600,000 or more is subject to estate taxes.

GETTING DOWN TO BUSINESS IN BLACK AND WHITE

The actual preparation of the will (preparing your own will is precarious) should be done by an attorney. Even the simplest of phrases can make a difference. If you don't use a professional in the legal field, you may not actually make things happen the way you had hoped.

Your attorney can help you make a lot of decisions, but the following decisions should be made by you alone:

WIDE ANGLE

A Word about Lawyers

Yes, it's true. For a formal will you don't **HAVE** to hire a lawyer—check your bookstore and computer software store for tools to help you. You can also fill out Living Trust paperwork and name a trustee. **BUT** using an attorney is the way to be most sure that your wishes will be carried out and protected according to the laws of your state.

If you don't use an attorney—make sure your will is signed, dated, and witnessed according to your state's requirements. (How do you find out what your state requires? The best way is to ask your attorney.)

One of the ways to find an attorney that suits your needs is by word of mouth. Talk to friends who have drawn up wills recently. Call a senior citizens' center (even if you aren't a senior citizen). Basically, ask around.

Many attorneys won't charge just to sit down the first time and talk about what you need to do in regards to estate planning. If you don't feel comfortable, try someone else.

Pay close attention to how well an attorney explains details to you. If he doesn't take care that you understand each step along the way, try someone else, even if you have already paid him something. Don't sign your will until you understand every provision.

Beware of doctors who tell you to leave the worrying to them. The same goes with lawyers. Your legal paperwork is ultimately your responsibility. Use a professional you can trust and make sure it is done right.

- Who is the executor, the person who will take responsibility for carrying out the wishes in your will? (Usually the executor is a close friend or family member. If your estate is complicated, for instance, if a family business is involved, the best executor may be a bank or institution. Remember to ask your executor before naming him/her officially in the will. This is NOT the place for a surprise.)
- Who are the beneficiaries? (Usually family and close friends designated in documents such as insurance policies)
- Who is the trustee of any trusts? (Someone able to manage finances for someone else)
- Who is the guardian of any minors who are in your care? (This is often the most difficult, but necessary. If there are any minors under your care, or guardianship, you will need to name a successor to that responsibility. You DEFINITELY need to ask their permission before naming them in your will.)
- What specific gifts of property are going to which person? (Every decision you make here will be one less decision your family and attorneys will need to make.)

CHOOSING BENEFICIARIES

A beneficiary is the person who will get the gift (or benefit) of your will. Most state courts consider beneficiaries to be the "natural objects of one's affection." For a parent this would mean children, grandchildren, close friends, a spouse.

   If you name any of these people as beneficiaries there is no reason for anyone to doubt your will. Keep in mind, though, that in some states a failure to leave a gift to one of these people is viewed with suspicion and should be supported in the will. You may want to at least mention them by name, for instance, "To them I leave my wishes for a good life." In this way the readers of your will don't have to wonder if you just forgot. There are also states that require a token gift to each family member.

Gifts to people outside of this group of close friends and immediate family can be viewed with suspicion. This would mean people like a girlfriend/boyfriend, dinner buddy, church friend, longtime bank teller. Your family (or a judge) may be concerned that someone outside of your family may have influenced you to withhold from your family. This happens sometimes to elderly people who don't have family close by. Your estate is certainly yours to do with what you will. But you might want to give a reason for gifts that you make to people outside of your family to show that the gift is deliberate and well thought out.

Review your legal documents at least every three to five years or anytime one of these events happens within your immediate family:

- Divorce and remarriage
- New grandchildren
- An increase or decrease in assets
- A relocation
- A death

Keep Two

Make sure someone knows where your legal documents are. It's a good idea to keep two copies in separate places. Tell two people their location. When you make a change in your documents throw away all copies but the current one so there will be no misunderstandings.

DON'T FORGET

ESTATE TRUST

One definition of a trust is a legal arrangement in which one person transfers ownership of assets to another person or corporation. Another, more colorful, definition is a legal vehicle to park assets for a specified time and distribute the income and principal in a specified way.

Whatever definition you use, someone must be appointed TRUSTEE to manage those assets for the benefit of someone else (the beneficiary). Who can be a trustee? An adult child or relative, a lawyer, accountant, or other professional, a bank or trust company.

There are three basic kinds of trusts:

1. The most common trust is one that simply places funds in trust for minor children until they get older. The trustee normally has the authority to distribute the funds to the children. Therefore, you want to be careful who you place as trustee. Most trusts are not under the control of courts. Therefore, if the trustee misuses or overspends the trust, the beneficiary has nothing but a legal right to sue the trustee once he or she becomes an adult.

2. A spendthrift trust protects the funds from overexpenditures. These overexpenditures can happen in several ways. In some cases this kind of trust protects the beneficiary from creditors. In other cases it protects the beneficiary from himself. The money is only distributed at specified times and at specified amounts. Usually with a spendthrift trust the actual funds are not subject to creditors. Only the funds that are distributed to the beneficiary are at risk.

3. Also, trusts are established for tax purposes. You'll hear of many

different kinds of tax shelter trusts including Q-TIP (Qualified Termi-nable Interest Property Trust), GRIT (Grantor Retained Interest Trust). Your attorney can talk with you about which kind of trust will work best for your situation. Very specific language must be used so an attorney is a key factor.

Wills and Trusts

Here are some terms you might hear as you talk with someone about wills and trusts.

AGENT: a person to whom you've signed over power of attorney

WIDE ANGLE

IRREVOCABLE TRUST: An irrevocable trust is one in which the donor does not share in the principal or the income of the trust and cannot demand the trust to be returned. Certain types of trusts must be irrevocable.

LIVING TRUST: a trust established while you are alive

NON-PROBATE ASSETS: assets that pass to a named beneficiary (like life insurance)

POA: power of attorney

PROBATE ASSETS: assets that pass to heirs through your will and the probate process

REVOCABLE TRUST: A revocable trust can be taken back. Whoever donated it can ask for it back. Therefore, it can be taxed upon your death because it was within your control.

TESTAMENTARY TRUST: a trust created in your will

TRUST: an arrangement of assets with guidelines for distribution and a trustee to oversee that distribution

To set up a trust you need to talk with a tax attorney. Don't make the mistake of talking to an accountant about estate planning. Accountants generally deal with accounts. Attorneys set up legal agreements and that is what a trust is.

POWER OF ATTORNEY

You can grant the power of attorney to someone else to legally act on your behalf. Granting the power of attorney (POA) to someone (making them the agent or attorney-in-fact) does not require that they be an attorney. You need to pick someone you trust, since you are

DON'T FORGET

Remember:

Every estate needs an executor.

Every trust needs a trustee.

Every minor needs a guardian.

giving them the power to make decisions that are legal and binding.

There are several different kinds of POAs.

1. Specific POA
This kind of POA is granted for a single purpose, for instance, the selling of a house. This kind of POA terminates if you become incompetent for any reason (for instance, a stroke).

2. General POA
This kind of POA gives broad authority to the agent to handle everything including decisions on medical care. This kind of POA also terminates if

you become incompetent for any reason. Check with your bank, brokerage firms, or other financial institutions as to whether they recognize a general POA. In order to have someone handle your business with them, you may need to institute a specific POA. If so, they should be able to make the forms available for you.

3. Durable POA
This kind of POA extends beyond a person's incompetence, allowing the holder of the power to continue to make decisions even though the grantor no longer has

Do-it-Yourself

THE BOTTOM LINE If you are committed to being a do-it-yourself-er as far as estate planning, remember that there are computer programs set up just for this purpose. To research this software you can search the web pages of your favorite software manufacturer or browse your computer store aisles. Another option is to check out the library. Often computer magazines list their software reviews in an index. Look up "Wills" or "Estate Planning" and see what's available.

capacity. This kind of POA is particularly helpful when a person has a progressive disease like Alzheimer's.

4. Springing POA
This is a variation of a durable POA. It comes into effect only upon the occurrence of a certain event. Most events which cause this kind of POA to spring in effect are incapacitating events such as entering a nursing home or losing physical or mental competence. By assigning this type of POA, you keep your own right to make choices about your life, but have provided for yourself when you are unable to do so. Many states that allow springing POAs require two doctors to confirm your status before allowing the POA to come into effect. This protects you from giving up control before it is necessary or you are ready.

Keep in mind that all POAs are extinguished at death. So even if you grant someone durable POA, when you die they lose power and your will is then the basis of all decisions made. The executor of the will and the trustee of any trusts, then, are the ones who have the power to carry out your wishes. Just because a person has your power of attorney, they

WOW!

Merry Christmas!???

When Tom Barton was in his late 50s he began to realize that he had left some details of his life unattended. There were conversations he wanted to have with his adult children. There were decisions he needed to make about which son would serve as the executor of his will. He could make a list a page long.

Unfortunately, though, as Tom began to prompt those conversations he either received a stiff shoulder, "Let's don't talk about those kinds of things, Dad," or a real-to-life drama, "Are you sick? Is there something I should know?" Because of this Tom decided to approach the issues in a broader context. For Christmas he gave each of his children an estate planning kit. He asked them to work through the initial checklist together as a family so they would each know something about the plans of the others.

His plan worked. In a setting where everyone of all ages was discussing some morbid eventualities, the pressure was relieved in dealing with Tom's burial wishes and living will. In this way Tom attended well to his own estate planning process as well as leading his family into a significant discussion about their future.

do not automatically become the executor of your will.

LIVING WILLS

A living will is a document that outlines your wishes in regards to what methods should be used or not used to keep you alive. Ultimately, the purpose of a living will is to prevent someone from having an undignified death. Their use grew out of the concern that while extraordinary measures are now available to doctors and hospitals that will keep someone "alive," the quality of that life and the cost involved may not be what that person would choose for themselves.

Each state has different requirements for living wills. In some states a living will can be overridden by the closest living relative. In some states, health care institutions are so bound by this document that if they have a

WIDE ANGLE

Planning is Worth It

The Bakers were a family of two divorced parents and four adult children. They had not given much thought to funerals or wills or estates until Billy, the second oldest son, died in the night. He didn't have a will. He hadn't expressed his wishes about burial to anyone, including his new wife. His sons were not provided for by the laws of his state unless their stepmother chose to do so, which she did not.

There were some difficult years for the Bakers as they sorted out Billy's estate and family. Once things had settled down, though, they began to ask each other questions about burial and possessions. They became aware of how each family member hoped his legacy would be cared for. When their father passed away the next year, they were more able to deal with their loss, rather than the legalities of it.

conflicting hospital policy, they'll send the patient on to a hospital that can adhere to the document rather than treat them. In some states a living will is only valid for five years.

Most hospitals have the forms readily available. Typically, though, living wills are very general. They will ask questions such as:

1. If you know your condition is terminal, do you want your doctor to employ extraordinary means to keep you alive?
2. If you are in a vegetative state, do you want your doctor to withhold artificial nutrition or hydration? (feeding tubes and intravenous fluids)

Whether your state requires you to refile periodically or not, it is a good idea to review your living will regularly. You may feel differently about these decisions at different stages in your life. The age of your children and other family members may figure into your decisions as well.

SECTION 14

PLACES TO RETIRE

PLACES TO RETIRE

TOUGH CALL OR NO-BRAINER?

Where do you want to retire? That sounds like a straightforward question, doesn't it? But it can have many layers and priorities fitted into a small space. WHERE you want to retire has to do with WHO you want to be near and what kind of CLIMATE you want to be exposed to and where you can AFFORD to live. But whether retirement is forty years away or next month, wishes and dreams

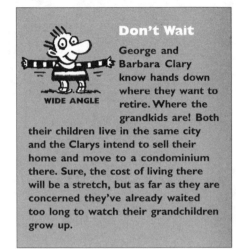

Don't Wait

George and Barbara Clary know hands down where they want to retire. Where the grandkids are! Both their children live in the same city and the Clarys intend to sell their home and move to a condominium there. Sure, the cost of living there will be a stretch, but as far as they are concerned they've already waited too long to watch their grandchildren grow up.

are still free. Whether you hope you go on an adventure or finally fix up that basement, the "where" question is a reality for you.

WHAT TO CONSIDER ABOUT THE LOCATIONS

Most of us spend our lives thinking about our geographical location in terms of job opportunities and family ties. Retirement is unique in that we often see it as our last hooray. Probably because it is! For that reason, it's good to examine options in your life that previously may have been unreachable. For instance, what kind of places suit you the most?

Rural Places

Plus Factors: a relaxed momentum, more of a sense of community, usually good housing costs, less crime and noise

Minus factors: banking services, hospitals, and entertainment are not usually cutting edge

Suburban Places

Plus Factors: the activities of the city nearby, but a little distance from the crowds and momentum, convenience

Minus factors: You'll need a car—things won't be within walking distance nor will mass transit do the trick, property taxes may be high

City Places

Plus Factors: close to cultural events and activities, continuing education, spectator sports, airports, libraries, mass transportation

Minus factors: housing costs can be higher, faster pace, ever-changing, noisy, higher crime rate

WOW!

Life Doesn't Have to Be Hard

Elliot and Amanda Schultz have worked hard all their lives. They raised five children in the same three-bedroom house. Now they are ready to sit back and relax. The house is paid for. The garden needs some attention. Puttering around there as well as volunteering at their church suits them just fine.

Places Abroad

Plus Factors: livings costs CAN be quite low, SS benefits will follow you, you can see places you've dreamed of, household help is more prevalent and less expensive

Minus factors: Medicare doesn't cross the border, the worth of your money fluctuates, medical care may be inferior, so much is unfamiliar, citizenship issues

No Place and Every Place (The Roving Lifestyle)

Plus Factors: you can keep your costs quite low, you see new places and things, you meet a lot of people, less responsibility than managing a home

Minus factors: small living space, "new" translates into "unfamiliar," medical care changes often, handling bills and other mail requires some attention

RETIRING TO A BEAUTIFUL PLACE

There are many beautiful places in this world to live. Which do you love the most? Where does your mind wander when your day is too stressful and you think of somewhere far away?

The Mountains

Whether it is the majesty of the Rockies or the quaint warmth of the Smokies, mountains appeal to the souls of some people. There

Pick Your Spot

Sam and Gay Bolin have always enjoyed socializing. Now that they are facing a retirement with some leisure time they are considering their options. The grandchildren are practically grown so they will soon be scattered. Most of their friends have moved out of their old neighborhood. The Bolins are looking closely at a retirement village in Florida with activities and a golf course. It sounds like a residence in a resort to them and they are ready.

WOW!

are plenty of places to live either in the mountains or accessible to the mountains. Here are just a few that have found their way onto some top retirement lists: Montana, Idaho, Colorado, and North Carolina.

The Beach

If you don't mind sand, and enjoy the sun and summer, maybe one of the coasts would be a good place for you. Some of the states you might consider are: coastal California, coastal Florida, North Carolina, South Carolina, and Georgia.

The Desert

New Mexico, Tucson, Arizona, West Texas

BEST PLACES IN THE COUNTRY TO RETIRE

There are a lot of lists out there. At your local library you can probably find at least five. Here are ten places that appear on most of them.

Look Out!

WIDE ANGLE

Nancy and Bill Klingle know exactly where they want to retire. EVERYWHERE! They've sold their home and moved into a small retirement village apartment. They used the extra money to buy a small camper-style van and are ready to hit the road. They've even considered crossing the border into Canada in the spring and Mexico in the winter. Look out retirement, here they come!

1. Tucson, Arizona: It's a "you name it, we've got it" kind of place with mountains and desert, universities and culture, a sense of history, and big-city convenience. The summers are hot, but dry. For some of the same, check out

Scottsdale and Prescott, Arizona.

2. Daytona Beach, Florida: Any place in Florida the sun is going to feel good to retired bones, but Daytona offers a lot more than warm weather. Daytona Beach is possibly America's most famous beach. If you want fun and sun, this is the place. The Daytona 500 is a big draw, not to mention Mickey Mouse town (Orlando) about an hour away. For some of the same, check out Ft. Lauderdale and Melbourne, Florida.

3. Ft. Myers, Florida: Ft. Myers tops several lists as the best place in the country to retire. Located on the gulf coast, Ft. Myers is a retiree-friendly city.

Food for Thought

CATCH A CLUE

A college town might be one of the worst places to retire if you want to work part-time. There are too many hungry college students that will work cheap.

Tucson, Arizona has been known to have more than 360 days of sunshine each year.

If your priority is on employment and leisure/entertainment, bigger cities come out ahead.

If your priority is on economy, housing, and personal safety, smaller places rate higher.

The most popular state in the U.S. in which to retire is Florida.

   In fact, the income of retirees has at times supplied about a third of the area income. For some of the same, check out Cape Coral, Tampa, and Naples, Florida.

4. San Diego, California: Good weather all year round, plenty of recreation, and ninety miles of beach all come together to make San Diego a great place to live if you like city life. You'll need to shop around for economical

housing, but the shopping will be worth it. For some of the same, check out Santa Barbara, California.

5. Austin, Texas: The terrain is rolling and green and the Colorado River runs through the middle of town. And did you know it's the state capital and the home of the University of Texas, to boot? The summers are hot, but there are some tax breaks and great health care facilities. Austin is a great place to work and to retire. For some of the same, check out San Antonio and Ft. Worth, Texas.

6. Colorado Springs, Colorado: Located at the foot of Pikes Peak, Colorado Springs attracts retirees and tourists alike. Good neighborhoods and health care facilities make it all the more appealing. It is a high-altitude city, which may have some ramifications for seniors with heart or lung problems, but short of that, this place is one "Ah" moment after another. For some of the same, check out Loveland and Ft. Collins, Colorado.

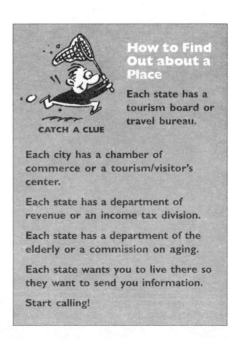

CATCH A CLUE

How to Find Out about a Place

Each state has a tourism board or travel bureau.

Each city has a chamber of commerce or a tourism/visitor's center.

Each state has a department of revenue or an income tax division.

Each state has a department of the elderly or a commission on aging.

Each state wants you to live there so they want to send you information.

Start calling!

7. Santa Fe, New Mexico: If economy is not your major concern Santa Fe is a great place to consider. It's an art

lover's haven as well as a sports enthusiast's dream. You would be at the foot of the Rockies with the history of Spanish and Native American cultures. For some of the same, check out Las Cruces and the outskirts of Albuquerque, New Mexico.

8. Coeur D'Alene, Idaho: You may not have thought of Idaho as a place to put on your list, but if you like winter and love snow, this could be a good place for you. There is plenty of activity during the summers, which are mild and dry. For some of the same, check out Kalispell, Montana.

9. Hot Springs, Arkansas: Arkansas is an economical place to live. Add to that the beauty of the Hot Springs area, the plentiful golf courses, and the Hot Springs National Park and you've found an ideal location to

WIDE ANGLE

Let's Talk Florida

There's just no getting around the fact that Florida is the most popular place to go for retirement. It's hot in the summer and the summer is long, but it abounds with beautiful weather and terrain and lots of other retired people to be with.

Florida divides into about six sections:
- the Panhandle or Northwest (Pensacola, Panama City, Ft. Walton Beach)
- the Historic Region or Northeast (Jacksonville, St. Augustine)
- the West Coast or Gulf Coast (Clearwater, St. Petersburg, Sarasota, Naples, the Everglades)
- Central Florida (Orlando, Lakeland, Ocala)
- the East Coast (Daytona Beach, Cape Canaveral, Melbourne)
- the Gold Coast or Southeast (West Palm Beach, Ft. Lauderdale, Miami)

Of course, the further south you go the hotter it becomes, but almost anyplace in Florida is a good place to find somewhere in the sun.

spend your time. This is a place where you make your own fun, but there is plenty of fun to be made. For some of the same, check out Fayetteville, Arkansas and Branson, Missouri.

10. Asheville, North Carolina: If you like snow, but not too much of it; if you like senior amenities, but other age groups too; if you like all four seasons, but none too overwhelming; and if you want access to the mountains, Asheville might be just the place for you. Depending on which way you drive, you can find about any level of sophistication or retreat that you need. For some of the same, check out Hendersonville and Brevard, North Carolina.

Some other cities you may want to research are:

1. Las Vegas, Nevada
2. Eugene, Oregon
3. Florence, Oregon
4. St. Petersburg, Florida
5. Traverse City, Michigan
6. Bellingham, Washington
7. Gainesville, Florida
8. Myrtle Beach, South Carolina
9. Panama City, Florida

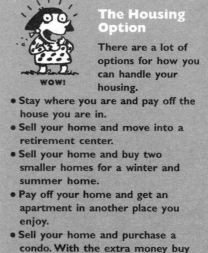

WOW!

The Housing Option

There are a lot of options for how you can handle your housing.

- Stay where you are and pay off the house you are in.
- Sell your home and move into a retirement center.
- Sell your home and buy two smaller homes for a winter and summer home.
- Pay off your home and get an apartment in another place you enjoy.
- Sell your home and purchase a condo. With the extra money buy an RV for traveling.

A RETIREMENT QUIZ

If you are married you may want to take this quiz alone and then compare your answers with your spouse's answers.

1. When I think of where I want to spend the rest of my life, the first relationship that comes to mind is
   1. my children
   2. my spouse
   3. friends

2. When I imagine myself walking in the front door of my retirement home I see
   1. the front door I walk into now
   2. an RV
   3. a multiple housing community

3. I am most relaxed at
   1. home
   2. a restaurant
   3. an event

4. I enjoy most being around people
    1. who I'm related to
    2. different than me
    3. my own age

5. When I think about retiring, my biggest concern is
    1. family ties
    2. boredom
    3. friends

Add up the sum of the numbers attached to the answers you chose. For instance, if you chose answer number one, add in one point.

If your answers totaled 9 or less:
You might consider retiring close to home.

If your answers totaled 10–14:
You might consider travelling a lot in retirement.

If your answers totaled 15–19:
You might consider moving to a retirement community.

SECTION 15
GOD AND YOUR RETIREMENT

GOD AND YOUR RETIREMENT

Because we know God meets us at every part of life, we know He meets us at retirement. Because we know God uses us in every stage of our lives, we know He uses us during our retirement. We often view our postemployment years as years of rest, forsaking the corporate ladder, but in terms of our spiritual growth, these years are years in which to bloom.

There is no pension plan for your spirituality. There's no nest egg that you have stored away in terms of your obedience and followship. There is no retirement plan in your role as God's disciple. He offers no social security other than the same hope that He's offered all along—seek Me and you will find Me, when you search with all your heart.

Even if you retire early, your

Turning Events

WIDE ANGLE

"My husband died a few years ago. I never imagined then that I would be travelling without him each spring to the Appalachian Mountains on a short-term missions project. But I do! With my team I help families repair their homes and teach the children Bible stories every day. I also help teach the young mothers about sanitation and child-rearing. When I retired, I knew I would do a lot of things, but I never imagined this would be one of them. But I'm glad...I really am."
—**Virginia, Nashville, Tennessee**

retirement is the closest place to heaven you've been yet. Think about retirement as a time to grow your relationship with God in new and deeper ways. Think about how you will serve Him differently than before.

"Moreover, when God gives any man wealth and possessions, and enables him to enjoy them, to accept his lot and be happy in his work—this is a gift of God. He seldom reflects on the days of his life, because God keeps him occupied with gladness of heart." Ecclesiastes 5:19–20

SHORT- AND LONG-TERM MISSIONS PROJECTS

Need Help?

You may want to write for:

The Short-Term Resources & Opportunities Catalog Distribution Central
P.O. Box 40519 Pasadena, CA 91114
Phone: (626) 798-8582

CATCH A CLUE

When you retire you face an opportunity to refocus your life. Your circumstances change. Your schedule changes. Your income often changes. You have occasion to invest your time differently than you did when you were working full-time. Nevertheless, the same scriptural guidelines prevail:

"Do not store up for yourselves treasures on earth, where moth and rust destroy, and where thieves break in and steal. But store up for yourselves treasures in heaven, where moth and rust do not destroy, and where thieves do not break in and steal. For where your treasure is, there your heart will be also." Matthew 6:19–21

"Provide purses for yourselves that will not wear out, a treasure in heaven that will not be exhausted, where no thief comes near and no moth destroys. For where your treasure is, there your heart will be also." Luke 12:33–34

Maybe you have been the kind of person who gave up a week's vacation to cook for summer camp or travel on a mission trip. Maybe you have been a person who traveled with your church group to help a missions team. Whether you did or not, once you are a retired person you may find that you have the time and interest to take part in missions like you never have before.

You may be surprised, though, at the colors and textures that missions take on these days. The world is a much smaller place and much more connected than in decades past. Computers now play a large role in missions organiza-

THE BIBLE SAYS

Love Each Other

"You are my friends if you do what I command. I no longer call you servants, because a servant does not know his master's business. Instead, I have called you friends, for everything that I learned from my Father I have made known to you. You did not choose me, but I chose you and appointed you to go and bear fruit—fruit that will last. Then the Father will give you whatever you ask in my name. This is my command: Love each other." (John 15:14–17)

tions and in denominations to keep track of missionaries, to help them translate the Word of God, and to keep them organized and in touch. A lot of the same skills you used in the workplace are the same skills a missions organization might need from you.

Here are some other things that may have changed about missions since you first started hearing about missionaries:

1. The rising need for computer hardware maintenance
2. The need to maintain centers on which groups of missionaries live
3. The need to provide more technical support to missionaries, even from U.S. locations by E-mail, for the increased technology that they use on the field

4. A concentration on people groups rather than just countries. Because of Bible translations people are grouped according to the language they speak rather than simply the country in which they live.

5. With the increase of immigrants in America, what we used to call "foreign" missions (influencing people of another culture), can happen right here at home.

Here is a sample list that you might see in terms of the needs that a mission organization has for short-term or long-term volunteers:

Project

"As soon as we both retired we went overseas on a two-year missions project to Brazil. It really changed our lives. I had never known anything but American Christianity, and my husband had only been out of the country once to Europe—and that was with the Navy. I never realized how fortunate we are to have the freedom we have in our nation as well as in Christ. We met people who were starving both physically and spiritually. We will probably go back again, but for a shorter amount of time."
—**Sylvia, Buffalo, New York**

Skills Needed:

- Accountants
- Administrators
- Bible teachers
- Builders
- Bookkeepers
- Carpenters
- Dentists
- Electricians
- Engineers
- Guest house managers
- Houseparents
- Laboratory technicians

- Librarians
- Maintenance technicians
- Mechanics
- Nurses
- Physicians
- Plumbers
- Schoolteachers
- Secretaries
- ...and many more!

Sounds like just about anyone can fit into that list, doesn't it? If you are interested in staying in the U.S. to volunteer for missions, you may work somewhere such as:

- a reservation
- a rural community
- a college campus
- an English-as-a-second-language course
- a church
- a homeless shelter
- a food bank
- a clinic
- a refugee organization

If you are interested in going overseas to volunteer in missions, here are some countries you may consider:

Afghanistan

Albania

Algeria

Armenia

Austria

Bangladesh

Belarus

Belgium

Bolivia	Libya
Bosnia	Macedonia
Brazil	Madagascar
Bulgaria	Malaysia
Cambodia (Kampuchea)	Mongolia
Cameroon	Morocco
Canada	Mozambique
Central African Republic	Nigeria
Colombia	North Korea
Croatia	Pakistan
Egypt	Papua New Guinea
Ethiopia	Philippines
Fiji	Romania
France	Russia
Germany	Saudi Arabia
Ghana	Senegal
Greece	Sierra Leone
Guinea	Singapore
India	Somalia
Indonesia	South Africa
Iran	Sri Lanka
Iraq	Sudan
Israel	Taiwan
Japan	Thailand
Jordan	Togo
Kenya	Tunisia
Kuwait	Turkey
Laos	Ukraine
Lebanon	United Arab Emirates
Liberia	Vietnam

Yemen
Yugoslavia
Zambia

And finally, if you are not going to be travelling with your own church group to do a mission project, these are some missions organizations that you might call about short-term opportunities.

- Africa Inland Mission
- Ambassadors for Christ International
- American Missionary Fellowship
- Arab World Ministries
- Belgian Evangelical Mission
- Big World Ventures
- Billy Graham Evangelistic Association
- Campus Crusade for Christ
- Child Evangelism Fellowship
- Christian Friends of Costa Rica
- Christian Veterinary Mission
- Christian World Mission
- Doulos International Ministries
- Emmaus Road International
- Flagstaff Mission to the Navajos
- Good News International
- Grace Ministries International

Productive Work

THE BIBLE SAYS

"Therefore go and make disciples of all nations, baptizing them in the name of the Father and of the Son and of the Holy Spirit, and teaching them to obey everything I have commanded you. And surely I am with you always, to the very end of the age." (Matthew 28:19–20)

- Greater Europe Mission
- His Place International
- InterVarsity Missions
- Mission Aviation Fellowship
- New Tribes Mission
- Operation Mobilization
- SEND
- SIM (Society for International Missions)
- Student Mobilization
- Teen Missions International
- UFM
- Women's Missionary Union
- Wycliffe Bible Translators
- Youth for Christ International
- Youth With A Mission (YWAM)

INVOLVEMENT AT CHURCH

Your own church is a great place to invest in eternal treasures. Whether you will still be attending your home church, or retiring to a new location and attending a new church, they will most likely always have opportunities for volunteers.

The difference between volunteering for a church and volunteering for a missions project can be great. On a missions project you are doing a specific task and your efforts are often obviously linked to that task. You can often literally see the need you are meeting. At your church your efforts might not have such an obvious link.

Modern churches often involve buildings and teaching supplies and equipment. Even though the long-range goal of the church is to teach the gospel and see the kingdom increased, part of doing that is just keeping the day-to-day operation running in good order. As a volunteer at church you may be cleaning out closets or organizing paints for preschoolers. Nevertheless you are contributing to the cause of Christ by supporting the ministries of the church.

What kinds of things can you do at church? Here are some suggestions:

- teach a Sunday school class
- visit sick members at home or the hospital
- new visitor follow-up
- assist the custodian in his daily and weekly duties
- work in the kitchen before or after fellowship meals
- assist in the office helping a staff member or a church secretary
- man an information desk
- make phone calls for staff members
- make copies
- help drive groups of children or adults
- stay in the nursery during a service
- lead a discussion group or prayer group
- make snacks for a youth meeting
- stuff envelopes
- clean up the lawn or the parking lot

One of the best ways to find out what type of volunteers might be needed is to call the church secretary and simply ask. If you already have an idea of how you would like to volunteer, talk to the staff member who would be most interested in your plans.

If you're talking about starting something new, be prepared to take responsiblity for it. Sometimes the church isn't the best place to come up with your own ideas and expect everyone to be gung ho about it. A church is usually working on some kind of plan, whether it is obvious or not. Church staff members are usually stretched about as far as they can go, in regards to time and energy. Your ideas might not fit into their plan *at that time* and they might not be as free as you think to change that plan at a moment's notice. It might be a great idea, but the staff member just can't keep one more plate spinning. Be prepared and tough-skinned. Go with a servant's heart. If your idea won't work right then, ask what you could do that will work then and do it graciously. You can bring your original idea up again later.

THE BOTTOM LINE

Make a Difference

"I had tried on several occasions to take part in the mentoring program at my church. The first few times it just wasn't a good fit. I cared about the people I was working with, but our lives were very different. I decided to try one more time and was paired with a frazzled, young mother. She reminded me of myself in my twenties, trying to keep up with three preschoolers, two in diapers. I thought to myself, 'Ah, now THIS spiritual journey I understand.' Suddenly translating my faith and experiences was a natural thing as I watched her face the same mountains that I had climbed. I would say to anyone interested in mentoring, keep trying until you find someone with a similar journey. You can make a difference."—Alice, New York City

BEING A SPIRITUAL MENTOR

No matter who you are, no matter what you have experienced, you have something to share with someone younger. It might be merely mistakes you hope they will avoid, but nonetheless your journey has left you with helpful hints that will help someone else along their way. It is your privilege. And, you probably know, according to the Scripture, it is your responsibility:

"Only be careful, and watch yourselves closely so that you do not forget the things your eyes have seen or let them slip from your heart as long as you live. Teach them to your children and to their children after them." (Deuteronomy 4:9)

"Teach the older men to be temperate, worthy of respect, self-controlled, and sound in faith, in love and in endurance. Likewise, teach the older women to be reverent in the way they live, not to be slanderers or addicted to much wine, but to teach what is good..." (Titus 2:2–4)

"And the things you have heard me say in the presence of many witnesses entrust to reliable men who will also be qualified to teach others." (2 Timothy 2:2)

"Even when I am old and gray, do not forsake me, O God, till I declare your power to the next generation, your might to all who are to come." (Psalm 71:18)

CATCH A CLUE

Wanted: You!

"I guess I had let my wife do the spiritual work in our family. I was always busy with a business trip or working late. When I retired I suddenly became aware of how involved she was in our church. In fact, I resented it at first. Then as I watched her I realized it wasn't just the church she was committed to...it was God Himself. Don't get me wrong—I had made a priority on tithing my pay and attending services, but that was about it. Now that I'm partially retired I realize that I should have given God more attention all these years. I'm realizing that He didn't just want my money or my ears on Sunday morning. He wants me! And I realize it's not too late. Whatever years I have left I'm glad I'll have time to get to know Him better and serve Him more."
—Dan, Redlands, California

Mentoring someone else can be as formal or as informal as you want it to be. It can be simply having lunch once a week or once a month and listening. It can be something like discipleship in that you hold each other accountable in your spiritual disciplines. It can be reading a book together and discussing it. It can be reading through a book of the Bible and sharing notes. Mentoring can take as many forms as you can imagine. But there are a few things that it should include:

1. At least two people spending time together

2. One person taking responsibility for investing in the other through listening, sharing, praying and, often, studying together

3. It works best with a time limit, for instance, meeting once a week for three months. You can renew your commitment again when the three months are complete if you choose to, but setting a limit helps you stay focused with an end in sight.

A Lasting Impact

WIDE ANGLE

"I had worked in the church all my life. I had done my turn in the nursery. I had made my sandwiches for the youth suppers. I had done it all. All a nominating committee member had to do was look my way and I was out the door. But now that my husband Carl and I have been retired a few years things are starting to look different to me. We traveled at first and did a lot of vacationing. After some time, though, we had seen what we wanted to see. Now it's nice to settle back into our church and community. It's nice to meet the young couples who are struggling the same way we used to. It's like God is refocusing my attention on the generation coming after us and what we can share that might help them along. Believe it or not, I even signed up for nursery duty last week. Now that I have time to think about what has mattered most in my life, giving some of myself seems like an easier thing to do."
—**Sarah, Mesa, Arizona**

4. An understanding that you are in this relationship to help and encourage each other but not to take responsibility for each other's commitment to God or to yourselves.

Local social service agencies often have mentoring programs. These will not be spiritual mentoring programs, but would work the same in terms of commitment and time frame. Ask your educational director or youth leader at your church if they have any kind of mentoring program in place. You have more to share than you think.

Words to Remember

THE BIBLE SAYS

King David was a warrior by trade, a king by appointment. He did great things and he made great mistakes. These are two of the prayers he prayed. You can use them as well as you come to know God more. Memorize these words and pray the same prayers as a Hebrew king who hoped that God would make something of his life.

Teach me your way, O Lord, and I will walk in your truth; give me an undivided heart, that I may fear your name. (Psalm 86:11)

Teach me to do your will, for you are my God; may your good Spirit lead me on level ground. (Psalm 143:10)

KNOWING GOD BETTER THAN EVER

Remember when you were a child and you looked at adults as finished products? You couldn't imagine that they still had fears and areas where they wanted to grow. But somewhere along the way (hopefully) you realized that human beings never stop needing to grow. You are not finished yet, whether you are about to retire or an old hand at retirement.

Most of your life you spent rushing down a river, like some kind of log flume ride with twists and turns and near misses. Then suddenly the river widens and you get to slow down a bit (life doesn't slow down, mind you, but hopefully you do). That is retirement.

While retirement is a wonderful time to enjoy leisure and to focus on relationships, it's also a time to process life and to face God honestly with your life. It is a time to weigh in the balance what really matters. It is a time to let God provide for you as you age and as you need and as you feel unsure. It is a time to know God better than ever, through His Word, through prayer, and through spending time deliberately in His presence.

> "My son, if you accept my words
>   and store up my commands within you,
>   turning your ear to wisdom
>   and applying your heart to understanding,
>   and if you call out for insight

WIDE ANGLE

Helping Others

I traveled a winding road.
It wasn't so easy, I had quite a load,
But still I kept walking ahead
Some days filled with joy, some days filled with dread.
And finally it seemed I arrived!
I sat in the grass, my worn backpack and I
And found that I had quite a view—
Way back, 'round the bend I could see quite a few
Travelers who labored to come the same way.
And so I called out, "You can make it!" I'd say,
"Watch that pothole! That corner! That hill is quite steep!
Now just keep your balance, ahead there's a leap!"
And before I could notice, my weariness gone,
My modest life's journey helped lead someone on.

and cry aloud for understanding,
and if you look for it as for silver
and search for it as for hidden treasure,
then you will understand the fear of the LORD
and find the knowledge of God.
For the LORD gives wisdom,
and from his mouth come knowledge and understanding."

(Proverbs 2:1–6)

"Search me, O God, and know my heart; test me and know my
anxious thoughts.
See if there is any offensive way in me,
and lead me in the way everlasting.

(Psalm 139:23–24)

"Teach me your way, O LORD, and I will walk in your truth; give me an
undivided heart, that I may fear your name." (Psalm 86:11)

Retirement is that time in life in which God prepares you more than ever to
go home. Let Him tie up the loose ends for you. Let Him grow you even
more into His holy child, redeemed not by your works, but by His grace.
Learn to hear Him as you never have before. Learn to serve Him as you
never have before, by letting Him lead you into opportunities of service.

SECTION 16

NEW OPPORTUNITIES FOR FAMILY ENRICHMENT

A WORLD OF POTENTIAL

Ah, the freedom of retirement! With the demands of your career behind you, you are free to devote your time, attention, and resources to the things that matter most in your life. Obviously, chief among these priorities is your family. Retirement affords you opportunities to connect with your family that were never possible before. You'll find a few of these opportunities listed below.

THE OPPORTUNITY TO ASSIST

Your grandson has a soccer game at 3:00. His younger sister has to get to piano lessons by 3:15 and then to a birthday party across town by 4:00. At 3:30, their older sister is scheduled to return home from camp and needs to be picked up at a church forty-five minutes outside of town. The family's two cars and two parents just aren't enough to get everyone where he or she needs to be. Whatever shall they do?

Never fear, it's retired grandparent to the rescue! If you're fortunate enough to live close to your children and grandchildren, you will likely have plenty of opportunities to lend a hand to your overscheduled family. Chauffeuring your grandchildren around will not only lighten the load of their parents, it will also keep you involved in their lives.

THE OPPORTUNITY TO TRAVEL

If you don't live close to your children and grandchildren, retirement gives you an excellent excuse for hitting the open road to visit them. If you have children scattered across the country, why not plan an ambitious journey to visit all of them? Spend a month on the road, stopping along the way to visit sites you've always wanted to see. If you prefer a quicker, more direct approach, start a tradition with your spouse of buying airline tickets for each other instead of Christmas gifts and anniversary presents. It's a great rationale for flying across the country to see your family.

THE OPPORTUNITY TO ENTERTAIN

If traveling is out of the question for you, bring your family to your house. Airline tickets or money for travel expenses make great stocking stuffers for your kids and grandkids. Make sure that when your family does come to visit, you're prepared for them. Beyond sleeping arrangements, find out what your grandkids' favorite foods and preferred forms of entertainment are. As much as possible, try to accommodate them so that their stay with you will be as enjoyable as possible.

THE OPPORTUNITY TO ORGANIZE

When was the last time you held a family reunion? Not a holiday get-together with immediate family, but a real reunion, complete with great-aunts, second cousins, and long-lost uncles. A great way to channel your postretirement time and energy would be to plan and organize a grand reunion.

If you should decide to undertake such a project, be warned: It's a tremendous amount of work. (Although, with the people-finding capabilities offered by many Internet providers, much of the work can be done at your own computer and telephone.) We should also be quick to point out that the end result of organizing a reunion is well worth the effort involved. Bringing a family together is not only a great way to reconnect with relatives you haven't seen in years, it's also a great way to give your kids and grandkids a sense of heritage and connectedness.

THE OPPORTUNITY TO REACQUAINT OR REPAIR

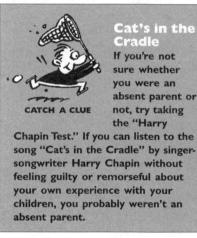

CATCH A CLUE

Cat's in the Cradle
If you're not sure whether you were an absent parent or not, try taking the "Harry Chapin Test." If you can listen to the song "Cat's in the Cradle" by singer-songwriter Harry Chapin without feeling guilty or remorseful about your own experience with your children, you probably weren't an absent parent.

The demands of a career can take their toll on a family. The feelings of resentment and even abandonment that result can take a long time to heal. While this is not the time to assign blame for such feelings, it is the time to discuss addressing them.

How often did your career take you away from your family? Were you an absent parent in the home? Do you know whether your children ever experienced bitter feelings because of the time you spent at work? These are tough questions that call for even tougher answers. It takes courage to admit that you may have erred on the side of workaholism when it came to balancing your priorities.

If you come to the realization that your career may have driven a wedge between you and your children, do your best to remove that wedge in retirement. Obviously, you can't make up for the time you've already lost; you can, however, work on making a fresh start. It won't be easy; it will take time. Fortunately for you, time is something you have in abundance as a retiree.

FINDING YOUR NICHE
WHAT IS A GRANDPARENT'S ROLE?

What are the qualities that make grandparents special? What are the roles that make them unique? What are the responsibilities that make a difference in the lives of their grandchildren? Here are a couple of suggestions for finding your niche as a grandparent.

Make yourself available as a listening resource.
Adolescents have no shortage of people talking to them. Most of the communication in their lives involves parents, teachers, coaches, and other adults telling them what to do. With all of this one-sided communication going on, is it any wonder that what most kids crave is someone who will listen to them? Why do you suppose they spend so much time on the phone every night?

If you really want to make a difference in your grandchildren's lives, become a great listener. Invite your grandkids to come to you when they need to be heard. And when they do come to you, show them the same conversational consideration that you would show an adult. Don't try to offer advice or give your opinions. Just listen. It may take some practice on your part, but when you truly learn to be a good listener, you'll find that your services are in regular demand.

Make your family history a part of your grandchildren's lives.

We're going to be brutally honest with you here. This won't be easy to do. Most teenagers would rather volunteer for root canals than listen to stories about "the old days." The quickest way to lose a teenager's attention is to begin a sentence with the words, "When I was your age. . ."

It's important for your grandchildren to have a sense of their family tradition and history. That's why you need to find creative ways to communicate that tradition. First, you must learn to lead with your best material. "Did I ever tell you about the time my father almost lost a foot trying to jump a train in Iowa?" That's an attention-getting opener. Of course, once you've got your grandkid's attention, you can throw in information about where your parents lived in Iowa, how long they stayed there, and why they left.

Second, you must know when to say when. Dole out your information and stories in bite-sized chunks. As any entertainer can tell you, it's always best to leave your audience wanting more.

Third, remember that repetition is the key to learning. Your grandkids will probably roll their eyes and sigh heavily when you try to tell them a story they've heard before. That's okay. Tell it again anyway. Those are the stories your grandkids will remember years later—the stories they'll pass on to their own kids.

ALL IN THE FAMILY
YOU AND YOUR CHILDREN

The concept is as profound as it is obvious: As long as you and your children are alive, you'll never stop being a parent. The dynamics of the relationship will change over time, but the fundamentals will remain the same. You will always be Dad (or Mom). He will always be Son. She will always be Daughter. And nothing can be done to change that.

Your retirement will give you time not only to reflect on your relationship with your kids but also to deepen it as well. Here are some tips to get you started.

Make peace
Chances are you've had some serious conflicts with your children over the years. Perhaps some bad blood exists to this day because of things that happened in the distant past. It's time to put those issues to rest once and for all. Think of your retirement years as the second half of your life, in which you set out to undo the mistakes you made (or allowed to escalate) in the first half. In making the peace, though, you should be willing to meet your children halfway (at least) in accepting responsibility for the conflict.

Have fun
You're never too old for father-son outings or mother-daughter days (or any other combination thereof). Just because you and children are both adults

now, it doesn't mean you can't take in ball games together or hit the links as golfing partners. Have fun together. Make plans to do the kinds of things that friends do.

Offer advice

One of the great things about being a parent is that no matter how old your child gets, you will always have more life experience than he or she does. Therefore, you always have a built-in justification for offering your opinions and advice. No matter what stage of life your child is in, you will have already experienced it and progressed beyond it. Chances are, you'll also have some useful advice for getting through each stage.

Seek advice

Few moments in life are as profound as the first time a parent seeks advice from his or her child. The affirmation, trust, and confidence that is communicated in that one simple gesture is guaranteed to swell the heart of any son or daughter, regardless of age.

So that there's no mistaking your intent, you should probably preface your request with a few heartfelt words of explanation. ("Your mother and I are facing a decision that we're nervous about. We need some level-headed, thoughtful advice, so naturally we thought of you.") You may be surprised by the positive response you get.

A GENERATION TWICE REMOVED

YOU AND YOUR GRANDCHILDREN

Though you're probably separated in age by at least forty years, you may be surprised at the relationship you can cultivate with your grandchildren—assuming, of course, that you're willing to work at that relationship. Toward that end, here are a few suggestions that might help you create a bond with your children's children.

GET ACQUAINTED WITH THEIR CULTURE

What kind of music do your grandchildren listen to? What kind of movies do they watch? Who are their favorite celebrities? What are the most pressing issues in their lives? Knowing the answers to these questions could go a long way toward establishing a bond with your grandkids. We're not suggesting that you start wearing concert T-shirts and blasting hard-core music while cruising around town. Even a passing knowledge of current trends and slang words might help you connect. At the very least, you'll be able to follow a conversation with your grandkids. What's more, the fact that you care enough to learn about the things they hold dear is bound to leave an impression on them.

DON'T EMBARRASS THEM

Embarrassment is the mortal enemy of all adolescents. The sooner you understand that, the better equipped you will be to establish a relationship with your grandkids that's comfortable for all of you. If your grandchildren even suspect that you're capable of embarrassing them, they will keep you at arm's length.

To gain their trust, you'll need to figure out what embarrasses them. Is it your fashion sense? Do you dress like an old person? (No offense intended.) Is it your sense of humor? Do you get a kick out of bad puns? Is it your personality? Are you prone to complaining about your kidney stones in front of perfect strangers? The process calls for a painfully honest self-evaluation.

We're certainly not suggesting that you buy a whole new wardrobe or radically change your personality to accommodate the whims of your grandchildren. What we are suggesting is that you do everything you can to eliminate barriers between you and your grandkids.

SHOW THEM RESPECT

Do you remember the first adult who ever took you seriously? The first person who seemed truly interested in your opinion? The first one who treated you like an adult? If you do remember the person, chances are those memories are fond ones.

How would you like to be that person in your grandchildren's lives? You can be, but it will take a concerted effort on your part. Lose the condescending attitude and start treating your grandkids and their opinions with the respect you'd give an adult. You may be surprised at how quickly your relationship with them improves.

SECTION 17
LEARN THE LINGO

THE "BOOMERIZATION" OF AMERICA

America is being "Boomerized" by the minute. Every seven minutes, someone, somewhere in this great country of ours, turns fifty. Put another way, Baby Boomers are coming of age.

This sectorized population explosion is heavily tilting America's demographics. According to the Census Bureau, the number of people younger than fifty has been declining since 1990 and will continue to do so until 2020; while the fifty-plus population will burgeon by 76 percent by 2020. Already, the eighty-five-plus group numbers 3.6 million, which is twenty-nine times larger than it was just seven years ago.

Given these staggering statistics, America is entering what some are calling a "retirement revolution," which is profoundly transforming the retirement and senior living landscape. This "revolution," without a doubt, is expanding the market for senior residential communities. No longer are active seniors willing to put up with long, bleak corridors, fluorescent lighting, and cold, iron handrails. No, sir. They want more exciting, deeply rewarding, and enriching living arrangements, and they're getting what they want. Here are some of the options:

Continuing Care Retirement Communities (CCRCs)
Continuing Care Retirement Communities incorporate assisted-living units on three levels: single-family residences, apartment living, and twenty-four hour nursing care. CCRCs usually are campus communities which offer seniors long-term contracts that guarantee lifelong shelter and access to specified health care services. In return, residents usually pay a lump-sum entrance fee and regular monthly payments. Depending

on the contract, the entrance fee may be nonrefundable, refundable on a declining basis over time, partially refundable, or fully refundable.

CCRC residents enjoy an independent lifestyle with the knowledge that if they become sick or frail, their needs will continue to be met. Most CCRCs establish minimum requirements for incoming residents based on age, financial assets, income level, and physical health and mobility. In general, residents are expected to move into the community while they are still independent and able to take care of themselves.

There are several basic types of CCRC contracts. Have an attorney review a CCRC contract before making any commitment.

- **Extensive contracts** cover shelter, residential services, and amenities, plus unlimited long-term nursing

THE BIBLE SAYS

James 1:27

That's what motivated Paul and Terry Klaassen to start a chain of assisted-living homes in 1996, called Sunrise Assisted Living. They bring to Sunrise, which went public in 1997, a blend of religious idealism and business pragmatism. "Our faith has been the biggest factor in shaping our operating philosophy," says Paul, an evangelical Christian.

And it appears that God is blessing the Klaassens. Sunrise is now one of the nation's most successful assisted-living companies, with thirty-eight residences in eleven states, and grossing more than $47 million in revenues a year. Sunrise's success is due, in part, to the atmosphere the Klaassens strive to maintain in all their homes: through carpeted floors, soft lighting, and chintz-print sofas—all reminiscent of the Victorian Era—and the intense training of Sunrise staff. The Klaassens try to hire employees who have "a servant's heart," meaning people who are truly dedicated to caring for others.

And why not? The Klaassens themselves set the precedent. "The care and feeding of frail widows," says Paul, "is cited in the Scriptures."
—*Forbes*, February 24, 1997

care without an increase in monthly payments (except for normal increases related to operating costs and inflation adjustments). An extensive contract spreads the risk of catastrophic health care costs among all the residents of a community, so that no single person faces financial ruin. Entrance fees and monthly costs under extensive contracts are typically higher than those under modified or fee-for-service contracts.

- **Modified continuing care contracts** cover shelter, residential services, and amenities, plus a specified amount of nursing care. After the specified amount of care has been received, the resident can continue to receive care on an unlimited basis but must pay for it at daily or monthly nursing care rates.

- **Fee-for-service continuing care contracts** cover shelter, residential services, and amenities. While emergency and short-term nursing care is usually included in the contract, access to long-term nursing care is guaranteed only at daily nursing care rates. Entrance and monthly fees are lower under this type of contract because residents are responsible for all long-term nursing and health care costs.

Request an information packet from every CCRC you are considering. Read it carefully. Visit each one. Dine with residents, talk with staff, read the residents' handbook. Assess the management's philosophy and its relationship with residents, keeping in mind your own needs.

Advice on evaluating a CCRC is offered in "The Continuing Care Retirement Community: A Guidebook for Consumers." To order, send a check for $4 to: AAHSA Publications, 901 E Street NW, Suite 500, Washington, DC 20004-2837. Allow up to six weeks for delivery.

ASSISTED LIVING COMMUNITIES (ALCS)

The term "assisted living" is defined by the Assisted Living Facilities Association of America as any group residential program that is not licensed as a nursing home and that provides personal care and support services to people who need help with daily living activities as a result of physical or cognitive disability. They are, therefore, designed for individuals who cannot function in an independent living environment but don't need nursing care on a daily basis. ALCs usually offer help with bathing, dressing, meals, and housekeeping. The amount of help provided depends on the individual's needs.

ALCs go by a variety of names: adult homes, personal care homes, retirement residences, and sheltered housing. ALCs are often affiliated with independent living communities or nursing care facilities, offering residents a continuum of care for changing needs. Many assisted living facilities also have professional nurses and other health care professionals on staff or available on-call should a resident require special care.

Most ALCs charge a monthly rent. In some cases, this fee covers only a few basic services; in others it is all-inclusive, covering a multitude of services. Some long-term care insurance covers assisted living, and some assisted living communities offer subsidies or other forms of financial aid on the basis of individual need. Applicants for subsidies are almost always placed on a waiting list.

In addition to visiting several communities and talking to residents and staff, it is important to do a careful comparison of fees and services. An all-inclusive fee that seems to be high at first could turn out to be more advantageous than a fee-for-service arrangement that combines a low basic rate with extra charges for the services you need.

To learn more about long-term care insurance that covers assisted living, contact United Seniors Health Cooperative (1331 H Street NW, Suite

WIDE ANGLE

Learn the Lingo

Active, or Independent, Retirement Communities offer richly rewarding relationships between peers, while at the same time maintaining the independent lifestyle of their active residents.

Activities of Daily Living (ADL) refers to those seniors who are able to maintain daily activities, such as dressing, eating, mobility, hygiene, grooming, shopping, laundry, etc.

Adult Day Care is a legally operated and licensed (if required in state) facility providing adult day care at least five days a week. It is not an overnight facility. It maintains records of services and a Plan of Care for each client; has established procedures for obtaining appropriate emergency medical aid; has contractual arrangements for providing the services of a dietitian, a licensed physical therapist, a licensed speech therapist, and a licensed occupational therapist; and maintains a staff that includes a full-time director, one or more nurses in attendance at least four hours per day, and enough full-time staff to maintain a client-to-staff ratio of eight to one or less.

Assisted Living Facility (ALF) refers to private apartments or suites, offering assistance with Activities of Daily Living (ADL).

Campus Communities are age-exclusive communities (usually 55+ or 62+) that are smaller (usually less than 1,000 residents), and primarily multihousing oriented (condo, apartment, duplex, etc.). Most have supportive services, and are referred to variously as Continuing Care Retirement Communities (CCRCs), Lifecare Communities (LCs), and Congregate Care Communities (CCCs). Some of the most outstanding ones are certified as Retirement Resorts.

Continuing Care Retirement Communities are Campus Communities (with supportive services) where residents pay a sizeable entry fee* and

Entry fee is usually partially or completely refundable. Policies differ widely so request written copies of sample resident agreements.

monthly fee. They then own a contract rather than actual property, and are able to enjoy a wide selection of services, features, and benefits. There are three types of contracts, which function like long-term care health insurance policies:
- *Extensive:* the most coverage, also known as Lifecare
- *Modified:* less coverage
- *Fee-for-Service:* the least coverage

Continuum of Care refers to the availability of supportive services at a Campus Community.

Dependent Living is the lifestyle focus of Supportive Communities. Residents live in close proximity to one another, meals are all provided, and twenty-four-hour access to assistance with ADLs is available.

Home Health Care refers to the provision of medical care and supportive services in the home.

Levels of Care refers to the three types of nursing care that is required by an individual.
- *Custodial:* assistance provided to help perform the activities of daily living
- *Intermediate Care:* requires occasional nursing or rehabilitative care from skilled medical personnel
- *Skilled (or Total) Care:* around-the-clock nursing and rehabilitative care that can only be provided by or under the supervision of skilled medical personnel, usually in a nursing home, although care may also be provided in the home

Lifecare Communities are Campus Communities that have a full supplement of supportive services available for residents, and where most residents are covered by an extensive Continuing Care Retirement Communities contract.

Long-Term Care (LTC) refers to assisted living and nursing facilities.

Medicaid is a federal government program that provides medical assistance to needy persons. It is not a program directed primarily to the elderly, but rather to the poor. It depends on financial need, low income, and low assets.

Medicare is a federal government program primarily designed to assist individuals age sixty-five and older. Eligibility is tied to Social Security eligibility and, unlike Medicaid, is not based on financial need, etc.

Note: Many people assume Medicare will cover most costs at a nursing facility. Not true. Only a minimal amount of nursing care is covered. Educate yourself, and purchase a LTC insurance policy, or move to a Campus Community that will provide coverage. Many seniors are financially devastated because they discover this too late.

Medigap is a Medicare supplemental insurance policy. Although Medicare covers many health care costs, you still have to pay Medicare's coinsurance and deductibles. There also are many medical services that Medicare does not cover. A Medigap policy provides reimbursement for the out-of-pocket costs that are not covered by Medicare and which are the beneficiary's share of health care costs. There are ten standard Medigap policies, and each offers a different combination of benefits.

Planned Communities are housing developments that primarily feature single-family homes, at least one clubhouse, and a wide variety of recreational amenities for community members to enjoy. The larger ones also have community shopping areas, as well as restaurants, banks, etc.

Respite Care allows a brief rest for those who would normally care for patients at home, such as family members. Respite Care must be provided by a licensed Respite Caregiver. The care can be provided in a hospital, nursing home, or assisted living facility.

Resort Retirement Communities is a fairly broad label referring to communities that have a resortlike appearance and location as well as a variety of recreational amenities for residents.

Retirement Communities is the label that has been used to describe huge seaside towns, as well as tiny ALFs, and absolutely everything in between. It has become a generic phrase and, therefore, has outlived its usefulness as a stand-alone identification label.

Retirement Resorts™ are Campus Communities that have been certified by ARRI because of outstanding recreational, educational, cultural, social, and spiritual features, and excellent on-site supportive services.

Skilled Nursing Facility (Nursing Home) is a facility under the supervision of a physician which provides continuous nursing services twenty-four hours per day by or under the supervision of a registered nurse, and maintains daily medical records on each patient.

Specialized Care Facilities refers to residential living facilities, specifically for those with Alzheimer's Disease or other forms of memory loss.

Supportive Services includes Assisted Living and/or Skilled Nursing Facilities (available in certain Campus Communities).

Ultra-Independent Living refers to those residents who live in regular towns or neighborhoods not part of a planned, campus, or supportive community.

Unrestricted Communities are individual towns and regions with more than one town that have special appeal for retirees, and are allocating resources to offer relocation information and assistance to retirees.

500, Washington, DC 20002; 202/393-6222), which publishes objective advice on how to buy long-term care insurance.

NURSING CARE FACILITIES (NURSING HOMES)

Nursing Care Facilities, or nursing homes, provide care for individuals who need nursing care on a regular basis but don't need to be hospitalized. The care is administered by nursing professionals under the direction of a physician. Many nursing care facilities also offer short-term or respite care for rehabilitation and other short-term needs.

Medicare, Medicaid, private insurance, and personal assets are all used under various circumstances to pay for services in a nursing care facility. If a facility is not certified by Medicare and Medicaid, the care will have to be paid for entirely with personal funds. In general, Medicare pays for skilled nursing care for a limited period of time following hospitalization for the same illness or condition. Medicaid, a government program for the indigent, covers nursing home care for individuals who meet strict medical and financial eligibility requirements. Some long-term care insurance pays for nursing home care; insurance payments are usually a fixed amount for a specified number of qualified days.

HOME CARE

Home Care is used primarily by those who are "ultra-independent," namely those who live at home but find it difficult to perform the most strenuous chores. Home Care, therefore, encompasses a wide variety of services—from intravenous therapy to snow shoveling. The services are intended to promote, maintain, restore, or minimize the effects of illness or disability. Home care services can be categorized as skilled care or home support services.

- *Skilled care* is service prescribed by a physician and provided by a licensed professional. Registered nurses and licensed practical nurses monitor medicines, help with wound or catheter care, teach the recipient or family members about special procedures, and provide other skilled services. Medical social workers provide short-term counseling and make referrals to community resources that can help recipients and their families cope with physical, emotional, and financial stresses. Nutritionists help plan special diets. Therapists perform physical, speech, respiratory, and occupational therapies in the home.

- *Home support services* include personal care (bathing, dressing, eating, exercising); homemaker services (meal preparation, light housekeeping, shopping); and companion ("sitter") services. Certified home health aides usually perform these services.

Following a hospitalization, Medicare pays for a limited number of physician-approved, home-care visits by skilled professionals, and, during the same period, for some ancillary support services. Medicaid coverage varies by state. Some private long-term health insurance covers home health care, but policies must be read carefully for definitions of skilled and unskilled care. In many cases, home care is paid for entirely out of private funds.

GERIATRIC CARE MANAGER

An evolving new specialty in the social services—the geriatric care manager—has been developed for the express purpose of helping families deal with the problems associated with caring for an older person. Geriatric care managers are health care professionals who have expertise in the aging process and in both health care and social services systems.

A geriatric care manager's work begins with a comprehensive assessment conducted by a registered nurse or a social worker. In addition to evaluating the older person's physical, functional, and emotional state and his or her current living arrangements, the care manager identifies and recommends community and private resources that might be helpful and provides ongoing monitoring and regular reporting if the client wishes.

The fees for these services range from $30 to $150 an hour. (The cost of any resources recommended are not included.) Some public and nonprofit agencies use a sliding-scale system based on income to set fees for their assessment and monitoring services.

A professional organization, the National Association of Professional Geriatric Care Managers, has established voluntary standards of quality and a code of ethics for geriatric care managers. The group represents care managers with professional degrees in human services and at least two years of geriatric experience. The National Association of Professional Geriatric Care Managers can refer managers who have the necessary professional credentials for membership and certification in the organization. The address is: NAPGCM, 655 N. Alvernon, Suite 108, Tucson, AZ 85711, (602) 881-8008.

ADULT DAY CARE CENTERS

Adult day care centers are not just cost-effective, they are also a positive way to prevent social isolation and mental deterioration that often accompanies isolation. Planned individual programs at adult day care centers encourage maximum participation by each person. The services provided by adult day centers generally include transportation to and from the home, one or two nutritionally balanced meals, outreach services to the community, and special programming.

Adult day care centers come in two distinctive forms:

The Right Questions

DON'T FORGET

If a family member needs adult day care services, there are some important things to consider. Visiting the care site and observing for at least an hour are most important. At that time, ask yourself the following questions:

1. What are the needs of the family and the member being referred?
2. Does the center provide services that match those needs?
3. Is the environment conducive to ensuring that the family member remains at his/her maximum level of independence?
4. Will the family member enjoy going there?
5. Would you enjoy going there?
6. Are the programs geared to the interests of older adults?
7. Are the participants treated with dignity?
8. Is the center clean?
9. Do staff actively interact with clients?
10. Are clients sitting alone or sleeping?

- *Social model centers* primarily attempt to alleviate feelings of loneliness and isolation among older adults, while fostering socialization and feelings of belonging. Services provided traditionally focus on recreational and social activity. These centers cater to adults whose physical condition is stable and who function independently in activities of daily living.

- *Medical model centers* provide health and rehabilitation services in addition to recreational services. The intent is rehabilitation or maintenance of each person's highest level of functioning and independence. Medical model facilities are traditionally staffed by health care professionals, and cater to those individuals in need of physical assistance or structured environments.

The cost of adult medical day care services are about half that of nursing home placement, averaging about $49 per day. Payment for adult day care services is not usually covered by insurance providers, although some of the newer long-term care policies do include provisions for this type of care. Medicare does not provide coverage, but some state Medicaid programs do.

INDEPENDENT LIVING COMMUNITIES OR ACTIVE RETIREMENT COMMUNITIES (ARCS)

Independent Living Communities, also known as Active Retirement Communities (ARCs) are, by far, the most popular for those individuals who are still active and want to maintain their independent, active lifestyle, but want the security of on-site health care services. Some independent living communities are affiliated with health care facilities that provide care when it is needed. Residents, however, can also purchase home health care services from outside providers.

Many independent living communities provide a full range of activities to promote social contact among residents. Shopping trips, outings to cultural events, and organized gatherings are typical activities. Many independent living communities also have tennis courts, swimming pools, activity rooms, and other amenities. Some may have their own golf course, but most do not and are situated close to public courses.

Most independent living communities are rental communities, but a few are townhome, condominium, or single-family communities in which residents must purchase their own units or homes. Costs and services vary widely. In some communities, a monthly fee covers many services, while in others a fee-for-service system is used.

A major question for those who are considering an ARC is: How will it meet my future health care needs? It is important to have a specific plan covering various contingencies.

Another question may be whether to select a fee-for-service arrangement or an all-inclusive fee. Fee-for-service may appear at first to be the more economical choice, but if a resident expects to use several of the available services, an all-inclusive fee could turn out to be a better buy. Consult your attorney before you make any permanent arrangements.

RETIREMENT RESORTS

If Active Retirement Communities are the most popular, than Retirement Resorts are a close second. Retirement communities are predominantly for the independently wealthy and active. These communities are homogenous, attracting people of the same age, interests, and financial

CATCH A CLUE

Retirement Bests and Worsts

Lowest Taxes
Alaska—No income or sales tax. Property tax exemption for those sixty-five and over.

Highest Taxes
New York—Highest combination of income, sales, and property taxes.

Most Public Golf Courses
Hilton Head Island, South Carolina

Most Affordable Housing
Lake Martin, Alabama

Least Affordable Housing
Carmel, California

Best Climate
Carmel, California

Worst Climate
McCall, Cascade, and Payetter Valley, Idaho

Lowest Percent of Population Sixty-five and Over
Alaska

Highest Percent of Population Sixty-five and Over
Florida

Lowest Doctor-to-Patient Ratio
Nevada

Highest Doctor-to-Patient Ratio
Washington, D.C.

Best Chances for Work
San Diego, California

Worst Chances for Work
Delta and Cedaredge, Colorado

Highest Cost of Living
Laguna Beach and Dana Point, California

Lowest Cost of Living
Hamilton and Bitterroot Valley, Montana

Fastest Growing Population
Riviera and Bullhead City, Arizona

Lowest Nursing Home Occupancy
Texas

Highest Nursing Home Occupancy
Mississippi

Lowest Property Crime Rate
Hiawassee, Georgia

Highest Property Crime Rate
Key West, Florida

background. They are ready-made social groups. Most seniors who move there do so because their friends already live there.

Though most of these country club-type communities are normally "gated" for security reasons, they do not offer on-site health care services. All of the residents are in good health, with their finances in order, and they don't want to be reminded that they're in their twilight years. Instead, retirement resorts are typically situated close to a metropolitan area, with hospitals and medical centers nearby.

These resorts are also chockfull of amenities, or are near enough for outside excursions to golf courses, lakes or oceans for fishing and boating, beaches, hiking trails, theaters and symphonies, parks and national forests, universities and colleges for continuing education and cultural experiences, gardens, tennis courts, swimming pools, bowling, beauty salons, shopping, and much, much more.

These seniors need never be bored. And usually never are. Some still travel extensively, as well, to Europe, or to Africa for safaris.

Retirement Resorts are fast becoming the most popular living arrangements among wealthy retirees. They're springing up all over America like wildflowers, and, as a result, migration patterns are swiftly changing. It used to be that Florida and Arizona were the traditional retirement destinations. Not so anymore. Now, the coastal states (the Carolinas, California, even Oregon and Washington) are in the running. North Carolina is the third most popular destination, with its year-round favorable weather and plethora of golf courses; while California ranks near the top for its climate, services, job opportunities, arts, and recreation.

There are also some key questions seniors need to ask themselves before they migrate.

- What type of climate do they prefer: hot and humid, hot and dry, or reasonably warm
- How far are they willing to move away from children and grandchildren?
- How close do they want to be to a city, airports, hospitals, and other amenities?
- How much can they afford for housing, taxes, utilities, health care, and traveling?

Investigate every cost associated with the resort; question carefully which amenities are included in the membership and which are not (i.e., greens fees, clubhouse fees, maintenance, etc.). Be extra careful before signing any contracts, and always consult your attorney.

DAYS ARE NUMBERED; SPEND THEM WISELY

Retirement can be looked upon with anticipation and joy. But, ultimately, it must be looked upon as a blessing, remembering that God has sustained you thus far in your earthly life, and that the rest of your days, which are numbered, should be used wisely.

The ultimate key, then, in chosing where to live and what to do after retiring is really *prayer*. "Let your requests be made known unto God" (Philippians 4:6, KJV). God is the ultimate sustainer of your life, and He will lead you to where He wants you to live out the end of your days, whether it's in your own hometown where you raised your children, or hundreds of miles away in the sunny climes of the South.

WIDE ANGLE

Fifty Fabulous Master Planned Retirement Communities in America

Most of the communities listed consist of single-family, detached homes, and/or townhomes (sometimes called villas or duplexes), condominiums, and apartments. The prices and square footage (s.f.) are ranges which include single-family homes, townhomes, condos, and apartments. You will need to call the particular ones you are most interested in for more information.

ALABAMA
Stillewaters Resort—Dadeville, AL
250-825-7021 or 888-797-3767
$70,000–$114,000 (800–1,500 s.f.)

ARIZONA
Sun City Grand—Surprise, AZ
800-341-6121
$100,000–$250,000 (1,110–2,900 s.f.)

Fairfield Homes Green Valley—
Green Valley, AZ
800-528-4930 or 520-625-4441
$89,000–$300,000 (985–2,550 s.f.)

Pebblecreek Resort Community—
Goodyear, AZ
602-935-6700 or 800-795-4663
$100,000–$200,000 (1,110–3,400 s.f.)

Saddlebrook Resort Community—
Tucson, AZ
520-825-3030 or 800-733-4050
$120,000–250,000 (1,330–3,497 s.f.)

ARIZONA, cont.
Sun Lakes Resort Community—
Chandler, AZ
602-895-9600 or 800-321-8643
$120,000–$250,000 (1,270–3,497 s.f.)

Bella Vista Village—Bella Vista, AZ
501-855-3776 or 800-228-7325
$79,000–$350,000 (1,200–3,500 s.f.)

Fairfield Bay—Fairfield Bay, AZ
501-884-3324 or 888-244-4386
$25,000–$350,000 (700–6,000 s.f.)

Holiday Island—Holiday Island, AZ
501-253-7810 or 800-643-2988
Sites: $70,000–$90,000

Hot Springs Village—Hot Springs, AZ
501-922-0250 or 800-451-4311
Sites: $5,000–$265,000

CALIFORNIA
Sun City Roseville—Roseville, CA
916-774-3500 or 800-633-5932
$120,000–$280,000 (968–2,619 s.f.)

Fifty Fabulous Master Planned Retirement Communities in America, cont.

CALIFORNIA, cont.
Leisure World Laguna Hills—Laguna Hills, CA
714-597-4360 or 800-711-9273
$49,000–$500,000 (900–2,600 s.f.)

Oakmont Village—Santa Rosa, CA
707-539-1611 or 888-625-6668
$150,000–$500,000 (1,200–3,500 s.f.)

Presley's Sun Lakes Country Club—Banning, CA
909-845-2123 or 800-368-8887
$100,000–$220,000 (1,266–2,250 s.f.)

Sonora Hills—Sonora, CA
209-532-3600 or 800-223-2346
$105,000–$134,000 (1,289–1,830 s.f.)

COLORADO
Heather Gardens—Aurora, CO
303-755-0652
$65,000–$210,000 (850–2,412 s.f.)

FLORIDA
The Country Club of Mount Dora—Mount Dora, FL
352-735-0115 or 800-213-6132
$130,000–$500,000 (1,580–6,000 s.f.)

Crescent Oaks—Tarpon Springs, FL
813-937-7661
$156,950–$300,000 (1,575–4,995 s.f.)

FLORIDA, cont.
Four Lakes Golf Club—Winter Haven, FL
941-299-4777 or 800-826-7076
$55,000–$120,000 (900–2,400 s.f.)

King's Point in Tamarac—Tamarac, FL
954-722-0121 or 800-233-6569
$120,000–$150,000 (1,830–2,272 s.f.)

Royal Highlands—Leesburg, FL
352-365-2303 or 800-325-4471
$100,000–$160,000 (1,151–1,925 s.f.)

Stoneybrook Golf & Country Club—Sarasota, FL
941-366-1611
$100,000–$300,000 (1,150–3,000 s.f.)

StrawBerry Ridge—Valrico, FL
819-689-9432 or 800-344-8995
$40,000–$110,000 (764–2,200 s.f.)

Timber Pines—Spring Hill, FL
352-629-8435 or 800-541-3111
$82,950–$170,000 (1,111– 2,321 s.f.)

The Villages of Citrus Hills—Hernando, FL
352-746-0527 or 800-323-7703
$80,000–$200,000 (1,500–3,000 s.f.)

Fifty Fabulous Master Planned Retirement Communities in America, cont.

FLORIDA, cont.
The Villages of Highlands Ridge—
Sebring, FL
841-471-1171 or 800-922-8099
$50,000–$170,000 (1,000–3,400 s.f.)

The Villages of Lady Lake—Lady
Lake, FL
352-753-2270 or 800-346-4556
$60,000–$300,000 (905–2,310 s.f.)

MARYLAND
Heritage Harbor—Annapolis, MD
301-261-8930
$99,000–$280,000 (900–2,500 s.f.)

Leisure World of Maryland—Silver
Spring, MD
301-598-2100
$130,000–$270,000 (888–1,496 s.f.)

NORTH CAROLINA
Albemarle Plantation—Hertford, NC
919-426-4653 or 800-523-5958
$80,000–$425,000 (700–4,000 s.f.)

Carolina Trace Country Club—
Sanford, NC
919-499-5121 or 800-227-2699
$80,000–$1.25M (1,400–6,000 s.f.)

Carriage Park—Hendersonville, NC
704-697-7200 or 800-639-8721
$145,000–$350,000 (1,800–4,000 s.f.)

NORTH CAROLINA, cont.
Cummings Cove Golf Community—
Hendersonville, NC
704-891-9412
$110,000–$500,000 (1,300–4,000 s.f.)

Fairfield Mountains—Lake Lure, NC
704-629-9111, ext. 2204
$85,000–$400,000 (1,200–4,000 s.f.)

Fairfield Sapphire Valley—Sapphire,
NC
704-743-7121
$65,000–$500,000 (700–10,000 s.f.)

Fearrington Village—Pittsboro, NC
919-542-4000 or 800-277-0130
$140,000–$400,000 (1,200–4,000 s.f.)

Knollwood Village—Pinehurst, NC
910-295-5011 or 800-633-8576
$50,000–$155,000 (850–2,200 s.f.)

Laurel Ridge Country Club—
Waynesville, NC
704-452-0545 or 800-433-7274
$120,000–$1M (1,300–12,000 s.f.)

OREGON
Claremont—Portland, OR
503-690-8512
$225,000–$338,000 (1,700–3,200 s.f.)

Fifty Fabulous Master Planned Retirement Communities in America, cont.

SOUTH CAROLINA

Sun City Hilton Head—Bluffton, SC
803-757-8700 or 800-978-9781
$100,000–$200,000 (1,039–2,856 s.f.)

Heritage Plantation—Pawleys Island, SC
803-237-9824 or 800-448-2010
$170,000+ (1,350–2,000 s.f.)

Keowee Key—Salem, SC
864-944-2200 or 800-537-5253
$52,000–$700,000 (1,000–7,000 s.f.)

Myrtle Trace—Myrtle Beach, SC
803-448-1045 or 800-227-0631
$120,000–$180,000 (1,400–2,000 s.f.)

Savannah Lakes Village—McCormick, SC
864-391-2151 or 800-442-2829
$90,000–$220,000 (1,200–5,000 s.f.)

Willbrook Plantation—Pawleys Island, SC
800-476-2861
$140,000–$650,000 (1,332–4,500 s.f.)

TENNESSEE

Fairfield Glade—Fairfield Glade, TN
615-484-7521
$50,000–$162,000 (1,200–2,800 s.f.)

Tellico Village—Loudon, TN
423-458-6822 or 800-646-LAKE
$120,000–$750,000 (1,000–6,000 s.f.)

TEXAS

Sun City Georgetown—Georgetown, TX
512-931-6900 or 800-833-5932
$100,000–$200,000 (1,120–2,900 s.f.)

VIRGINIA

Ford's Colony at Williamsburg—Williamsburg, VA
757-258-4000 or 800-334-6033
$170,000–$2M (1,360–8,000 s.f)

WASHINGTON

Providence Point—Issaquah, WA
206-392-2300 or 800-648-1818
$115,000–$325,000 (850–2,700 s.f.)

Source: *50 Fabulous Planned Retirement Communities for Active Adults,*
by Bob Greenwald.

Check Out the Chambers

THE BOTTOM LINE

Before you move to your desired destination, you might want to contact that state and/or town's Chamber of Commerce. Chambers of Commerce are great resources of information about that state or town's community affairs, business and economic development, recreational and entertainment life, and much more. Here is a listing of the Chambers of the states most favored for retirement.

Alabama Department of Economic & Community Affairs
P.O. Box 5690
Montgomery, AL 36103
800-235-4757

Arizona Chamber of Commerce
1221 E. Osborn, #100
Phoenix, AZ 85014-5539
602-248-9172

Phoenix Chamber of Commerce
Loraine La Morder, Info. Spec.
201 N. Central Avenue, #2700
Phoenix, AZ 85073
602-254-5521

Fayetteville (AR) Chamber of Commerce
P.O. Box 4216
Fayetteville, AR 72720
800-766-4626 or 501-521-1710

California State Chamber of Commerce
P.O. Box 1736
Sacramento, CA 95218
916-444-6670

Check Out the Chambers, cont.

Colorado Association of Commerce & Industry
1776 Lincoln Street, #1200
Denver, CO 80203
303-831-7411

Florida Chamber of Commerce
P.O. Box 11309
Tallahassee, FL 32302
904-425-1200

Maryland Chamber of Commerce
60 West Street, #100
Annapolis, MD 21401
410-269-0642

North Carolina Citizens for Business & Industry
P.O. Box 2508
Raleigh, NC 27602
919-836-1400

State of North Carolina, Commerce Department
Travel & Tourism Division
430 N. Salisbury Street
Raleigh, NC 27611
919-733-4171

State of Oregon, Economic Development/Tourism Manager
775 Summer Street NE
Salem, OR 97310
503-373-1270

South Carolina State Chamber of Commerce
1201 Main Street, #1810
Columbia, SC 29201
803-799-4601

Check Out the Chambers, cont.

State of South Carolina, Parks/Recreation & Tourism Dept.
1205 Pendleton Street, #248
Columbia, SC 29201
803-734-0135

State of Tennessee, Economic & Community Development Department
320 6th Avenue N, 8th Floor
Nashville, TN 37243
615-741-1888

State of Texas, Commerce Department
Tourism Division
P.O. Box 12728
Austin, TX 78711
512-936-0100

Texas Association of Business & Chamber of Commerce
P.O. Box 2989
Austin, TX 78768
512-477-6721

State of Virginia, Commerce Trade Office
Housing & Community Development Dept.
Jackson Center
501 N. 2nd Street
Richmond, VA 23219
804-371-7025

Virginia Chamber of Commerce
9 S. Fifth Street
Richmond, VA 23219
804-644-1607

Check Out the Chambers, cont.

State of Washington, Community Trade
& Economic Development/Tourism Division
P.O. Box 48300
Olympia, WA 98504
360-753-5795

State of Washington, State Parks & Recreation Commission
Public Affairs Division
P.O. Box 42650
Olympia, WA 98504
360-902-8501

SECTION 18
COUNTDOWN TO RETIREMENT

A COUNTDOWN TO RETIREMENT

For the sake of this countdown we'll assume you're going to retire at age sixty-five. Here are some landmarks to help you prepare.

60 YEARS TO GO (ABOUT AGE 5)

This is probably one of the few times in your life when you don't have to be concerned about retirement at all…really. What with walking, talking, first day at kindergarten and learning manners, your plate is rather full. If you'll notice though, you're learning the very skills that you'll need when you retire, so learn them well.

You can hope that you're parents are starting a college/future/savings fund for you now, but don't hold it against them if they don't. They've got a lot to be thinking about too. (See forty years to go and thirty years to go.)

50 YEARS TO GO (ABOUT AGE 15)

About now you're thinking about the opposite sex…a LOT. That's a lot to handle, so retirement doesn't need to be a priority. Learn all you can, though, because it won't be any easier to understand the opposite sex when you retire than it is now. You think that's impossible? Ignorance is bliss.

Pay a lot of attention when you are learning to drive. You may not always have this privilege, so enjoy it while you can still drive fast and feel good about it.

40 YEARS TO GO (ABOUT AGE 25)

You're probably either starting your career or getting yet another degree. While retirement seems a long way off, it should come into your mind. When you interview for a job you should be hearing about the retirement plans involved. Pension should be a word in your vocabulary. It's really good if you hear your employer is going to "match" your contribution in any kind of plan. Make sure you understand (in this changing world) how the retirement dollars you earn in each job will be treated when you leave that job or when you use some of the funds.

- Start a filing system for your financial documents and other important papers.
- If you haven't yet, learn to balance your bank statement.
- If you don't have a savings account, start one.
- Learn to keep up with receipts and to understand your yearly tax return.
- Make a simple will.
- If you're single, get enough life insurance to cover your debts and funeral expenses. Let your parents or next of kin know about your arrangements.
- If you're married, buy more life insurance, preferably a whole life policy.
- If you're already starting a family, name guardians for your children.
- It's OK to work hard, but start some habits for spending time with your family.

Getting your legal documents in order now lays the foundation that you can adjust and build on the rest of your life. Chances are your estate is simpler right now than it will be in the future. If you get some basic legal and financial categories set in your mind and in your filing cabinet now, then you'll have a better chance of keeping your estate in order as it grows.

30 YEARS TO GO (ABOUT AGE 35)

If you haven't done any of the things listed under "forty years to go" go ahead and start all of them now. Let someone besides your spouse know where your documents are, now that they are probably adding up. Write a will. Buy life insurance. Make sure it's whole life insurance so that you're investing in something that will pay you back.

- Review your legal documents and adjust them according to family and financial changes.
- If you haven't established a retirement fund of any kind by this point, start putting pressure on yourself.
- Besides checkings and savings accounts you should have some monies yielding higher interests that are working for you.
- Check in with your spouse in terms of where you both thought you would be by this point and how where you are measures up.
- If your life is made up only of work and kid stuff, start a new hobby that you and your wife can do together.

20 YEARS TO GO (ABOUT 45)

Again, if you still haven't done all of the things listed before now, it's not that scary; just sit down with a list and start. Don't beat yourself with a stupid-stick yet, but get going.

- Again, review any documents (wills, trusts, policies) that you've had in the file drawer for a while. Has your family structure changed at all? Are the provisions you've outlined in those documents affected?

- If you are still using a very simple, general will that served you well two decades ago, you may want to start getting more specific now.
- If you haven't done it already, consider a living will. Let your family know how you want the decisions handled if you should become unable to sustain life on your own.
- Sit down with a financial planner and get suggestions for how to get your finances in even better order.

10 YEARS TO GO (ABOUT AGE 55)

There are people who get this far with no preparation whatsoever toward retirement. If you are one of them, look at that stupid-stick over in the corner, but leave it there. Start from the beginning and get your life in order in terms of the legal documents that you should have current and the financial preparations that you should be making for fixed-income living.

Let's Put Your Savings into Perspective

Check out the approximate amount you'll save if you put back $50 a month...

WIDE ANGLE

At this interest	for 5 yrs	for 10 yrs	for 15 yrs	for 20 yrs
6 percent	$3,500	$8,500	$15,000	$22,500
8 percent	$3,700	$9,200	$17,000	$29,600
10 percent	$3,900	$10,300	$21,000	$38,200

If you'll notice, the key is in saving the money consistently for a long time. Can't do $50? Try $25. Try $10. Just try, and let it add up to an easier retirement.

- Review your will and any other estate documents to make sure they make the kind of provisions you want for yourself and your family. Review your living will as well.
- Review your assets. Sit down with a financial planner if you have never done that. Let them evaluate your position and make some suggestions. Are there any ways the assets you do have can be working harder for you? Is there stock that can be invested more wisely?
- If you don't have one, find a kind of exercise that you can enjoy into old age and begin to do it.
- Start spending some intentional time with your spouse. Really look at him or her. Work at communicating. Hold hands. In about ten years you'll be staring each other in the face quite a lot. Start now to invest in each other so that you'll enjoy those years filled with so much togetherness.
- Develop both a hobby that you enjoy alone and a hobby that you and your spouse can pursue together.

5 YEARS TO GO (ABOUT AGE 60)

It's really, really time to get ready.

- If you aren't already, start reading and educating yourself more about the options that retirement will afford you. Subscribe to some periodicals directly related to retirement.
- If you've been handling your estate yourself, sit down with a lawyer or CPA (whichever is appropriate for your needs) to determine if your estate is in order and accomplishing what you had hoped.
- Call your Social Security office and ask them how much your monthly check will be. Begin to compare your current expenses to that amount. Get an understanding of what kind of difference that is going to make.

- Also, get an idea of what expenses you'll be giving up when you retire. You won't be commuting. You won't be eating out for business lunches. You won't be paying out to Social Security.
- Talk with your spouse about his or her hopes and dreams for retirement. Even if you've talked about it before, things change, people change.
- Start researching the kind of living arrangements you would like to have as a retiree. Do you want to stay in the same house? Do you want to stay in the same city? Do you want to live in an RV? Do you want to travel at all?
- If you've enjoyed an office at work, start preparing a space at home for you to work or read or simply to *be*.
- Get an understanding of what will change about your insurance coverage when you retire. Medicare is not meant to be all-inclusive, so search out your options. Talk to your friends who are retired. Learn from their mistakes. Join an HMO or purchase private insurance such as Blue Cross/ Blue Shield.
- Do some reading about elderly care facilities. Understand at least the categories and definitions of facilities so that you'll know what your options are as you face the aging process ahead.
- If you haven't been going to the doctor regularly, start. Get a good handle on both your health and your spouse's. Educate yourself on any chronic conditions you will need to manage.

RETIREMENT: HAVE A GREAT TIME!

Whether you are prepared or not, breathe deeply, remember to smile, and find the good in the days afforded you. Find a way to give something back. Work a little if necessary.

INDEX

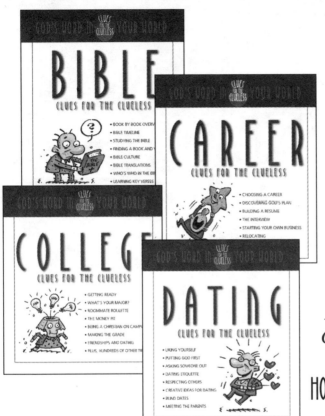